Comedies

Ludvig Holberg

Contents

INTRODUCTION 7
JEPPE OF THE HILL OR THE TRANSFORMED PEASANT ..16
ACT I 18
ACT II 33
ACT III 44
ACT IV 52
ACT V 63
EPILOGUE 74
THE POLITICAL TINKER 75
ACT I 77
ACT II 89
ACT III 102
ACT IV 114
ACT V 131
ACT V 143
ERASMUS MONTANUS OR RASMUS BERG 157
ACT I 159
ACT II 172
ACT III 186
ACT IV 208
ACT V 223

COMEDIES

BY

Ludvig Holberg

INTRODUCTION

Ludvig Holberg is generally considered the most remarkable of Danish writers. Though he produced books on international law, finance, and history, as well as satires, biographies, and moral essays, he is chiefly celebrated for his comedies, which still--nearly two hundred years after then composition--delight large audiences in Denmark, and bid fair to be immortal. These comedies were the fruit of the author's actual experience; they are closely related to his other works and reflect the range and diversity of his pursuits. To understand fully Holberg's creations, one must first become acquainted with the events of his life.

Ludvig Holberg was born in Bergen, December 3, 1684, of good parentage on both sides. His mother was a granddaughter of a distinguished bishop, and his father an army officer who had risen from the ranks by personal merit. Bergen had long been a trading-post of the Hanseatic League, and in the seventeenth centurv was distinctly cosmopolitan in character. Perhaps as a result of his environment, Holberg seemed early to have acquired a desire to travel. In any case, he devoted most of the years of his young manhood to seeing the woild.

In 1704, shortly after receiving his degree at the University of Copenhagen, he made a journey to the Netherlands. About a year later, he went to England, where he spent more than two years, partly in Oxford and partly in London, studying history and absorbing new ideas. In

1708, as the tutor of a young Danish boy, he visited Dresden, Leipzig, and Halle. Soon after his return to Copenhagen, he obtained a small stipend in a foundation for students, called Borch's College, While there he wrote two historical treatises of enough value to win him an appointment as "extraordinary" professor in the university. Though this position gave him the right to the first vacancy that might occur in the faculty, it did not entitle him to any salary, and it was only through the good offices of a friend at court that he obtained a stipend of about $150 a year for four years, during which time he was to be a sort of travelling fellow of the university. In the spring of 1714, Holberg, then thirty years of age, left Copenhagen for his fourth journey abroad.

This excursion was far more extensive and picturesque than any he had undertaken before. He travelled first to Paris, by way of Amsterdam and Brussels, and later to Genoa and Rome, by way of Marseilles. Except for the necessary sea voyages, most of the journey was made on foot. After staying in Rome for six months, harassed the entire time by malarial fever, he turned his face towards home. In order to escape the discomforts and perils of travel by sea, he decided to return to Paris overland, and walked from Rome to Florence in fourteen days. Finding his health improved by the regular exercise, he continued on foot over the Alps to Lyons, and subsequently to Paris and Copenhagen, where he arrived in the autumn of 1716. Holberg had gone abroad to satisfy his keen intellectual curiosity; he remained to study in foreign lands, and to observe life as a philosopher and artist. Without his seemingly aimless years of wandering, he might conceivably have become an able historian; he could hardly have developed his brilliant talent for satire and comedy.

When Holberg returned home, he found no vacancy in the faculty. While waiting in penury for the death of some professor, he wrote one of his most successful works of scholarship, an Introduction to International Law. At last, in December, 1717, he inherited, as it were, the chair of metaphysics in the university, being thus forced to begin his academic career by teaching a subject that he held in contempt. Fortunately this situation was not permanent. In 1719, he became professor of Latin; in the following year, a member of the university council; later in life, professor of history, the subject he liked best; and finally he was elected treasurer of the corporation. Holberg was thus associated all his life with academic pursuits. The greater part of his intellectual work was devoted to regular university duties and to the composition of scholarly treatises and moral essays, while the writing of the comedies that won him permanent fame formed but a short interlude in his busy life. He became a dramatist almost by chance.

In 1721, some influential citizens of Copenhagen decided that the time was ripe for establishing native drama in Denmark. A company was formed under the direction of a cashiered French actor, Montaigu, who obtained royal permission to bring out plays in Danish. Holberg, having become well known by his mock-heroic poem Peder Paars, was at once invited to furnish the company with original comedies, and responded enthusiastically. For the next few months he wrote with almost incredible swiftness, and by the time the theatre was opened, on August 23, 1722, he had finished five of his best plays, among which were Jeppe of the Hill (Jeppe paa Bjerget) and The Political Tinker (Den politiske Kandestober). During the six years in which the company eked out its precarious existence, Holberg produced twenty-six comedies, most of which were successfully performed. His literary fecundity seems the more remarkable when it is remembered that he had no Danish models.

The theatre was not well supported by the public. After the first year, the receipts of an evening amounted to no more than $13, and sometimes the actors were compelled to tell the spectators who had gathered that they could not afford to present the play to so small an audience. In 1728, the company was at last granted a royal subvention of about $2500 a year by Frederick VI, and it had begun to play under the proud title of Royal Actors, when Copenhagen was swept by a devastating fire. The theatre itself was not destroyed, but the town was so badly impoverished that for the moment all forms of public amusement had to be discontinued. Furthermore, the pietists, to whose doctrines the crown prince was a devout adherent, asserted that the fire was God's scourge for the wickedness of Copenhagen, the most impudent form of which, they believed, was the drama. Before conditions in the city were enough improved to warrant the resumption of his subsidy to the actors, the king died, on October 12, 1730. Under the reign of his pietistic successor, Christian VI (1730-1746), no dramatic performances of any sort were sanctioned; the theatre building was sold at auction, the company disbanded, and Holberg ceased writing plays.

In the year of Christian VI's accession to the throne, Holberg was made Professor of History at the university. Pietist though he was, the new monarch was an enthusiastic patron of scholarship, and during his reign Holberg devoted himself almost exclusively to research, particularly for his History of Denmark, on which his present reputation as an historian rests. The one important work of pure literature that he produced at this time was his Niels Klim's Subterranean Journey (1741), written in Latin, and published in Leipzig to evade the Danish censor. It is an account of a series of visits that Niels Klim pays to certain strange nations within the hollow of the earth. Like Robinson Crusoe, its partial prototype, it contains much pointed satire on the customs of contemporary society. It was soon translated into most other languages of Europe, and it is one of the very few among Holberg's works that have been put into English in any form.

At the death of Christian VI, in 1746, the obscurantist character of the court immediately changed. One of the first forms of amusement to be restored was the Danish theatre. Although Holberg had no official connection with the actors, he seems to have agreed to advise them about their repertory, and soon his association with the stage revived his inteiest in dramatic composition. During the year 1751-52, he wrote six new plays, but they lacked the spirited criticism of contemporary society which gave life to his earlier work. They are either founded on Latin models, or are heavily didactic plays, in which the author's humor fails under the burden of the moral.

The latter part of Holberg's life was spent in peace and affluence. His interests were more and more devoted to his large estates, and particularly to improving the conditions under which his own peasants labored. In 1747, he was elevated to the rank of baron, after bequeathing his estates to the crown to endow the old academy at Soroe. He died on January 28, 1754, and was buried in the abbey church of Soroe, beside the great Bishop Absalom.

The plays in this volume will give a fair idea of Holberg's best work. They are all domestic comedies of character, in which the foibles of some one central figure are held up to ridicule, particularly as they are revealed in his relations with a well-defined family group. The scene in such comedies, usually the home of a peasant or a member of the bourgeoisie, is pictured with uncompromising realism. Holberg insisted that his audiences should see everything that he saw. If a Danish peasant actually lay at times in a drunken stupor on a dunghill, he saw no reason why Jeppe should not appear on the stage in an equally disgusting condition.

If a peasant girl in life was not averse to simpering vulgarity, why should Lisbed talk any more circumspectly to Erasmus Montanus? Holberg, however, had none of the interest of the modern scientific naturalist in analyses of motive and conduct. His sense of fact was, therefore, picturesque rather than profound. Yet he never wasted his accurate realism upon insignificant things. Vulgar facts invariably led beyond themselves to situations of universal interest and significance.

"Jeppe of the Hill" is a very old story The original version is found in the "Arabian Nights," and it has been told over and over again. Shakespeare embodies it in "The Taming of the Shrew," and seven other versions occur in Elizabethan literature alone. This hackneyed farce, amplified by material from Biedermann's "Utopia," Holberg made the vehicle of profound delineation of character Dr. Georg Brandes says of Jeppe, "All that we should like to know of a man when we become acquainted with him, and much more than we usually do know of men with whom we become acquainted in real life or in drama, we know of Jeppe. All our questions are answered." [Footnote: "Om Ludvig Holbergs Jeppe paa Bjerget,"] We know not only how he has lived, but even how he will meet death. Jeppe possesses enough of the common stuff of human nature always to awaken comprehension and delight; yet he is more than an extraordinarily complete and convincing individual, and his story is more than an amusing farce. Widely prevalent social conditions of a past time are here expressed in human terms of lasting truth and vitality. In Jeppe the peasant of the eighteenth-century Sjaelland lives for all time.

The Political Tinker, while it contains no such deep study of personality as Jeppe of the Hill, is no less clearly a comedy of character and no less obviously a good human satire. In it the foibles of the central figure are displayed more definitely in their relation to the rest of his family. [Footnote: The play is probably founded upon the story of the political upholsterer which appears in an essay of The Tatler. For a general discussion of Holberg's relations to foreign literature, the reader is referred to The Comedies of Holberg, by O. J. Campbell, Jr. (Harvard Studies in Comparative Literature, vol. iii, Harvard University Press, 1914). This is the only full treatment of Holberg in English. Ed.] "The satire," says Holberg, in his introduction to the first published edition of the play, "is directed against those boasters among common people in free cities who sit in taverns and criticise the mayor and Council; they know everything and yet nothing.... I doubt if any one can show me a comedy more honorable and more moral.... The comedy, besides, is not less merry than moral, for it has kept spectators laughing from beginning to end, and for that reason, of all my comedies, it is played with the greatest profit for those concerned." The word "moral" as applied to this work illustrates the somewhat unusual meaning which Holberg attaches to it. Though he is continually at pains to speak of his "moral" comedies, it is manners and not morals that he satirizes. He is interested, not so much in effecting a fundamental reform in the lives of his characters, as in giving them a little social sense. He preaches, not against distinct moral turpitude like hypocrisy and avarice, but against inordinate affection for lap-dogs (Melampe), pietistic objections to masked balls {Masquerades}, and superstitious belief in legerdemain (Witchcraft). Holberg voices the urbane humanistic spirit that characterized the eighteenth century at its best.

Erasmus Montanus seems at first sight a mere farce, in which the author ridicules academic pedantry and the vapid formalism of logic as once taught at the University of Copenhagen. But it is much more than that. Holberg gives us a memorable series of genre paintings of Danish life of his day, and at the same time presents a situation of universal interest. Erasmus is a prig who has adopted some new ideas, not so much from righteous conviction as from the feeling that they will give him intellectual caste. His revolutionary theories raise an uproar in the village. Each apostle of the old order opposes them in his characteristic way, and Erasmus has not enough real faith within himself to prevail against the combined attacks of the Philistines; he renounces with oaths the assertions that the world is round. Still, there is nothing tragic in his renunciation, for we feel that he is as great a fool as any one in the play. Erasmus Montanus is a pure comedy, in which the author's humor plays freely upon all the figures in the drama; and it is just because the characters rather than the action absorb our interest that we do not regard it as a farce. Professor Vilhelm Andersen correctly described it as a "Danish culture-comedy of universal significance."

Holberg is often called the Danish Moliere. It is true that he learned many lessons of technique from the great trench dramatist, and borrowed freely and often from his work; but he differs from Moliere both in the quality of his humor and in the spirit that animates his critical view of life. He might as justly be called the Danish Plautus, or the Danish Spectator. The truth is, not only that Holberg possessed a profoundly original comic spirit, but also that his work is clearly related to many dramatic and literary traditions besides those of French comedy, notably to the commedia dell'arte, and the essays of The Tatler and The Spectator. Out of these various and diverse elements, nevertheless, he contrived to construct dramas at once original and national.

In a large sense, Holberg's comedies arc closely related to the rest of his work. His treatises, histories, essays, satires, and comedies are all diverse expressions of one definite purpose. Holberg's early life and natural cosmopolitan interests made him a citizen of eighteenth-century Europe, as a whole, and he strove steadily to bear the intellectual light of that urbane age to his native country, then backward in culture. Holberg--professor, scholar, and philosopher--seized with avidity the opportunity to write comedy, not from a desire to display his own versatility, or from an absorbing devotion to the drama as a form of art, but because he believed that through his plays he could fulfil most completely what he conceived to be his intellectual mission.

OSCAR JAMES CAMPBELL, JR.

May 20, 1914

JEPPE OF THE HILL OR THE TRANSFORMED PEASANT [JEPPE PAA BIERGET] A COMEDY IN FIVE ACTS 1722

DRAMATIS PERSONAE

JEPPE OF THE HILL, a peasant.

NILLE, his wife.

JACOB SHOEMAKER, an innkeeper.

BARON NILUS, lord of the district.

Secretary to the Baron.

ERIC, a lackey.

A Valet.

MAGNUS, the village gossip.

A Judge, two Lawyers, two Doctors, a Bailiff and his Wife, Lackeys, Retainers, and others.

ACTS I, IV, AND V

SCENE: A village road; on the left, Jeppe's house; on the right, Jacob Shoemaker's inn. The court in Act IV is held in the open, and a tree is used for the gallows in Act V.

ACT II

A bedroom in the Baron's castle.

ACT III

Dining-room in the same.

ACT I

SCENE I

(Nille, alone.)

NILLE. I hardly believe there's such another lazy lout in all the village as my husband, it's as much as I can do to get him up in the morning by pulling him out of bed by the hair. The scoundrel knows to-day is market-day, and yet he lies there asleep at this hour of the morning. The pastor said to me the other day, "Nille, you are much too hard on your husband; he is and he ought to be the master of the house." But I answered him, "No, my good pastor! If I should let my husband have his way in the household for a year, the gentry wouldn't get their rent nor the pastor his offering, for in that length of time he would turn all there was in the place into drink. Ought I let a man rule the household who is perfectly ready to sell his belongings and wife and children and even himself for brandy?" The pastor had nothing to say to that, but stood there stroking his chin. The bailiff agrees with me, and says, "My dear woman, pay no attention to the pastor. It's in the wedding-service, to be sure, that you must honor and obey your husband, but it's in your lease, which is more recent than the service, that you shall keep up your farm and meet your rent--a thing you can never do unless you haul your husband about by the hair every day and beat him to his work."

I pulled him out of bed just now and went out to the barn to see how things were getting along, when I came in again, he was sitting on a chair, asleep, with his breeches--saving your presence--pulled on one leg; so the switch had to come down from the hook, and my good Jeppe got a basting till he was wide awake again. The only thing he is afraid of is "Master Eric," as I call the switch. Hey, Jeppe, you cur, haven't you got into your clothes yet? Would you like to talk to Master Eric some more? Hey, Jeppe! Come in here!

SCENE 2

(Enter Jeppe.)

JEPPE. I've got to have time to get dressed, Nille! I can't go to town like a hog without my breeches or my jacket.

NILLE. Scurvy-neck! Haven't you had time to put on ten pairs of breeches since I waked you this morning?

JEPPE. Have you put away Master Eric, Nille?

NILLE. Yes, I have, but I know mighty well where to find him again, if you don't step lively. Come here!--See how he crawls.--Come here! You must go to town and buy me two pounds of soft soap, here's the money for it. But see here, if you're not back on this very spot inside of four hours, Master Eric will dance the polka on your back.

JEPPE. How can I walk four leagues in four hours, Nille?

NILLE. Who said anything about walking, you cuckold? You run. I've said my say once for all, now do as you like. [Exit Nille.]

SCENE 3

JEPPE. Now the sow's going in to eat her breakfast, while I, poor devil, must walk four leagues without bite or sup. Could any man have such a damnable wife as I have? I honestly think she's own cousin to Lucifer. Folks in the village say that Jeppe drinks, but they don't say why Jeppe drinks: I didn't get as many blows in all the ten years I was in the militia as I get in one day from my malicious wife. She beats me, the bailiff drives me to work as if I were an animal, and the deacon makes a cuckold of me. Haven't I good reason to drink? Don't I have to use the means nature gives us to drive away our troubles? If I were a dolt, I shouldn't take it to heart so, and I shouldn't drink so much, either; but it's a well-known fact that I am an intelligent man; so I feel such things more than others would, and that's why I have to drink. My neighbor Moens Christoffersen often says to me, speaking as my good friend, "May the devil gnaw your fat belly, Jeppe! You must hit back, if you want your old woman to behave." But I can't do anything to protect myself, for three reasons: in the the first place, because I haven't any courage; in the second, because of that damned Master Eric hanging behind the bed, which my back can't think of without blubbering; and thirdly, because I am, if I do say it who shouldn't, a meek soul and a good Christian, who never tries to revenge himself, even on the deacon who puts one horn on me after another. I put my mite in the plate for him on the three holy-days, although he hasn't the decency to give me so much as one mug of ale all the year round. Nothing ever wounded me more deeply than the cutting speech he made me last year: I was telling how once a savage bull, that had never been afraid of any man, took fright at the sight of me; and he answered, "Don't you see how that happened, Jeppe? The bull saw that you had bigger horns than he, so he didn't think it prudent to lock horns with his superior." I call you to witness, good people, if such words would not pierce an honorable man to the marrow of his bones. Still, I am so gentle that I have never even wished my wife dead. On the contrary, when she lay sick of a jaundice last year, I hoped she might live; for as hell is already full of bad women, Lucifer might send her back again, and then she'd be worse than ever. But if the deacon should die, I should be glad, for my own sake and for others' as well, for he does me nothing but evil and is no use to the parish. He's an ignorant devil, for he can't sing a note, much less mould a decent wax candle. Oh, but his predecessor, Christoffer, was a different sort of fellow. He had such a voice in his time that he sang down twelve deacons in the Credo. Once I started to quarrel openly with the deacon, when Nille herself heard him call me a cuckold. I said, "May the devil be your cuckold, deacon!" But what good did it do? Master Eric came right down off the wall to stop the quarrel, and my back got such a drubbing that I had to ask the deacon's leave to thank him, that he, as a well-educated man, should do such an honor to our house. Since that time I haven't thought of making any opposition. Yes, yes, Moens Christoffersen! You and the other peasants can very well talk, because your wives haven't any Master Eric hanging behind the bed. If I had one wish in the world, it would be either that my wife had no arms, or that I had no back. She may use her mouth as much as she pleases. But I must stop at Jacob Shoemaker's on the way--he'll surely let me have a pennyworth of brandy on credit--for I must have something to quench my thirst. Hey, Jacob Shoemaker! Are you up yet? Open the door, Jacob!

SCENE 4

(Enter Jacob Shoemaker, in his shirt.)

JACOB. Who the dickens wants to get in so early?

JEPPE. Good morning to you, Jacob Shoemaker.

JACOB. Thank you, Jeppe! You are up and about bright and early to-day.

JEPPE. Let us have a pennyworth of brandy, Jacob!

JACOB. With all my heart, when you show me the penny.

JEPPE. I'll give it to you when I come back here tomorrow.

JACOB. Jacob Shoemaker doesn't give credit, I know you must have a penny or two about you to pay with.

JEPPE. Honestly, Jacob, I have nothing but what my wife gave me to spend in town for her.

JACOB. You can easily beat them down a few pence on what you buy. What is it you're to get her?

JEPPE. I have to buy two pounds of soft soap.

JACOB. Why, can't you tell her the soap cost a penny or two more than you give for it?

JEPPE. I'm so afraid my wife would find out about it, and then I'd be in trouble.

JACOB. Nonsense! How could she find out? Can't you swear that you paid out all the money? You're as stupid as an ox.

JEPPE. That's true, Jacob! I can do that well enough.

JACOB. Out with your penny.

JEPPE. Here you are, but you must give me a penny change.

JACOB (coming in with the glass; drinks to him). Your health, Jeppe!

JEPPE. What a lot you take, you rogue!

JACOB. Oh, yes, but it's the custom for the host to drink his guest's health.

JEPPE. I know it is, but bad luck to the man that started the custom. Your health, Jacob!

JACOB. Thanks, Jeppe! You'll drink the other pennyworth next, so there's no use your troubling about change. Or do you want a glass to your credit when you come again? For I give you my word I haven't any change.

JEPPE. I'm damned if I do! If it's got to be spent, it might as well be spent now, so that I can feel I have something under my belt; but if you drink any of it, I won't pay.

JACOB. Your health!

JEPPE. God save our friends and ill befall our enemies. That does my belly good. Um-m-m.

JACOB. Good luck on your way, Jeppe.

JEPPE. Thanks, Jacob Shoemaker. (Exit Jacob.)

SCENE 5

(Jeppe feels happy and begins to sing.)

A white hen and a speckled hen
Got into a row with a rooster--

Oh, if I only dared drink another pennyworth! Oh, if I only dared drink another pennyworth! I think I'll do it. No, ill will come of it. If I could once get the inn out of my sight, I shouldn't need to; but it's as if some one were holding me back. I've got to go in again. But what is this you are doing, Jeppe? I seem to see Nille standing in my path with Master Eric in her hand. I must turn round again. Oh, if I only dared drink another pennyworth! My belly says, "Do it;" my back, "Don't." Which shall I obey? Isn't my belly bigger than my back? I think it is. Shall I knock? Hey, Jacob Shoemaker, come out here! But that cursed woman comes before my eyes again. If she only didn't break the bones of my back when she beats me, I'd let her go to the devil, but she lays on like ... Oh, God help me, miserable creature! What shall I do? Control your nature, Jeppe! Isn't it a shame to get into trouble for a paltry glass of brandy? No, I shan't do it this time; I must go on. Oh, if I only dared drink another pennyworth! It was my undoing that I got a taste of it; now I can't get away from it. Go on, legs! May the devil split you if you don't! Marry, the rogues won't budge. They want to go back to the inn. My limbs wage war on each other: my belly and my legs want to go to the inn, and my back wants to go to town. Will you go on, you dogs! you beasts! you scurvy wretches! The devil take them, they will go back to the inn; I have more trouble getting my own legs away from the inn than I have getting my piebald horse out of the stable. Oh, if I only dared drink another pennyworth! Who knows but Jacob Shoemaker might trust me for a penny or two, if I begged enough? Hey, Jacob! Another twopenny glass of brandy!

SCENE 6

(Enter Jacob)

JACOB. Hello, Jeppe! back again? I thought you had had too little. What good is a farthing's worth of brandy? That's hardly enough to wet your whistle.

JEPPE. That's so, Jacob! I'll spend another farthing! (Aside.) Once I've got it down, he'll have to trust me whether he wants to or not.

JACOB. Here's your farthing's worth of brandy, Jeppe, but money first.

JEPPE. You certainly can trust me while I'm drinking, as the proverb says.

JACOB. We don't give credit on proverbs, Jeppe! If you don't pay up, you won't get a drop; we have sworn off trusting any one, even the bailiff himself.

JEPPE (weeping). Can't you really trust me? I'm an honest man.

JACOB. No credit.

JEPPE. Here's your twopence, then, you beggar! Now it's done, drink, Jeppe! Oh, that goes to the right spot.

JACOB. It certainly does warm a man's insides.

JEPPE. The best thing about brandy is that it gives you courage. Now I don't think any more about my wife or Master Eric, I've been so changed by that last glass. Do you know this song, Jacob?

> Heir Peder and Kirsten sat at the table, Peteheia!
> Said all the bad words that they were able, Polemeia!
> In summer the happy starlings sing, Peteheia!
> May devil take Nille, the dirty thing, Polemeia!
> One day I went out upon the grass, Peteheia!
> The deacon, he is a hangman's ass, Polemeia!
> On my dappled horse I ride to the east, Peteheia!
> The deacon, he is a nasty beast, Polemeia!
> If you would know my wife's real name, Peteheia!
> I'll tell you: it is Lust and Shame, Polemeia!

I made up that song myself, Jacob!

JACOB. The devil you did!

JEPPE. Jeppe's not as dull as you think: I've also made up a song about shoemakers, which goes like this:

The shoemaker sits with his big bass viol, Philepom, Philepom!

JACOB. You poor fool, that's about a fiddler.

JEPPE. So it is. See here, Jacob! Give me twopence worth more of brandy.

JACOB. All right; I see you're a good fellow; you don't grudge spending a penny or two in my house.

JEPPE. Hey, Jacob! make it fourpence.

JACOB. Certainly.

JEPPE. (singing again).

> The earth drinks water,
> The sea drinks sun,
> The sun drinks sea,
> Everything on earth drinks;
> Why not me?

JACOB. Your health, Jeppe!

JEPPE. Mir zu!

JACOB. Here's to you in half of it!

JEPPE. Ich tank you, Jacob. Drink, man, and the devil take you and welcome!

JACOB. I see that you can talk German.

JEPPE. Yes, I have for a long time, but I don't like to except when I'm full.

JACOB. Then you must speak it at least once a day.

JEPPE. I was ten years m the militia, don't you think I ought to understand the language?

JACOB. I know, Jeppe! We were in the same company for two years.

JEPPE. So we were; I remember it now. You were hanged once when you ran away at Vissmar.

JACOB. I was going to be hanged, but I was pardoned. A miss is as good as a mile.

JEPPE. It's too bad you weren't hanged, Jacob! But weren't you with us at the auction on the heath--you know the one?

JACOB. Why, where wasn't I with you?

JEPPE. I never shall forget the first salt the Swedes made. I think 3000 men--or even 4000--fell all at once. Das ging fordeviled zu, Jacob! Du kannst das wohl rememberen. Ich kan nicht deny dass ich bange war at dat battle.

JACOB: Yes, yes, death is hard to face; a man always feels pious when he goes against the enemy.

Jeppe. Yes, that's so. I don't know how it happens. For I spent the whole night before the auction reading the Qualms of David.

JACOB. I wonder that you, who have been a soldier, should let yourself be browbeaten by your wife.

JEPPE. I? If I only could have her here now, you'd see how I should drub her! Another glass, Jacob! I still have eightpence, and when that's all drunk up I shall drink on credit. Give me a mug of ale, too. (Sings.)

> In Leipzig war ein Mann,
> In Leipzig war ein Mann,
> In Leipzig war ein lederner Mann,
> In Leipzig war ein lederner Mann,
> In Leipzig war ein Mann.
>
> Der Mann sie nahm ein Frau--

JACOB. Your health, Jeppe!

JEPPE. Hey! he--y! he--y!

> Here's to you, and here's to me,
> And here's to all the company!

JACOB. Won't you drink the bailiff's health?

JEPPE. Sure enough; give me credit for another penny-worth. The bailiff is an honest man; when we slip a rix-dollar into his fist, he'll swear to his lordship that we can't pay our rent. Now I'm a villain if I have any more money; you must trust me for a farthing or two.

JACOB. No, Jeppe, you can't stand any more now. I'm not the kind of man to let his patrons force themselves to drink more than is good for them. I'd rather lose my trade than do that. It would be a sin.

JEPPE. Just another farthing's worth!

JACOB. No, Jeppe, you can't have any more. Just think what a long way you have to walk.

JEPPE. Cur! Carrion! Beast! Scoundrel! Hey, hey, h--e--y!

JACOB. Good-bye, Jeppe! Good luck to you!

[Exit Jacob.]

SCENE 7

JEPPE. Oh, Jeppe, you are as full as a beast! My legs don't want to carry me. Will you stand still, you carrion? Let's see, what time is it? Hey, Jacob, you dog of a shoemaker! I want another drink. Will you stay still, you dogs! May the devil take me if they will keep quiet. Thank you, Jacob Shoemaker! I'll have another. Listen, friend! which way does the road to town go? Stand still, I say! See, the brute is full. You drank like a rogue, Jacob! Is that a farthing's worth of brandy ... You pour like a Turk. (As he speaks, he falls and lies on the ground.)

SCENE 8

(Enter Baron Nilus, Secretary, Valet, Eric, and another Lackey.)

BARON. It looks as if we were going to have a good harvest this year; see how thick that barley is growing.

SECRETARY. True, my lord, but that means that a barrel of barley won't bring more than five marks this year.

BARON. That makes no difference. The peasants are always better off in good seasons.

SECRETARY. I don't know how that may be, my lord, but the peasants always complain and ask for seed-corn, no matter whether the year is fruitful or not. When they have something, they drink so much the more. There is an inn-keeper who lives near here, called Jacob Shoemaker, who helps a good deal to keep the peasants poor; they say he puts salt in his ale to make them thirsty so they will drink more.

BARON. We shall have to drive the fellow out. But what is that lying in the road? It must be a dead man. One hears of nothing but misfortune nowadays. Run and see what it is, one of you!

LACKEY. That is Jeppe of the Hill, whose wife is such a terror. Get up, Jeppe! No, he wouldn't wake even if we pummelled him and pulled his hair.

BARON. Let him be, then. I want to play a little joke on him. You are usually full of ingenious ideas. Can't you think of something to divert me?

SECRETARY. I think it would be good fun to tie a paper collar round his neck, or else cut off his hair.

VALET. I think it would be more amusing to smear his face with ink and then send some one to see how his wife takes it when he comes home in that condition.

BARON. That's not bad. But what do you wager that Eric won't hit on something better still? Let's hear your suggestion, Eric.

ERIC. My idea is that we take off all his clothes and put him in my lord's best bed, and in the morning when he wakes, all of us treat him as if he were the lord of the domain, so he won't know how he has got so transformed. And when we have convinced him that he is the baron, we can get him drunk again, as he is now, and lay him on the same dunghill in his own old clothes. If all this is skilfully carried out, it will work wonderfully, and he will imagine that he had dreamt of his good fortune, or has actually been in paradise.

BARON. Eric, you're a big man and therefore you have big ideas. But what if we should wake him in the process?

ERIC. I'm sure we shalln't do that, my lord! for this same Jeppe is one of the heaviest sleepers in the whole district. Last year they tried setting off a rocket under his head, but when the rocket went off he never even stirred in his sleep.

BARON. Then let us do it. Drag him right off, put a fine shirt on him, and lay him in my best bed.

ACT II

SCENE I

(Jeppe is lying in the baron's bed with a cloth-of-gold dressing-gown on a chair beside him. He wakes up, ruts his eyes, looks about, and becomes frightened; he rubs them again, puts a hand to his head, and finds a gold-embroidered nightcap on it; he moistens his fingers and wipes out his eyes, then rubs them again, turns the nightcap around and looks at it, looks at the fine shirt he is wearing, at the dressing-gown and the other fine things in the room, making strange faces. Meanwhile, soft music begins to play, and Jeppe clasps his hands and weeps. When the music stops, he speaks.)

JEPPE. What is all this? What splendor! How did I get here? Am I dreaming, or am I awake? I certainly am awake. Where is my wife, where are my children, where is my house, and where is Jeppe? Everything is changed, and I am, too--Oh, what does it all mean? What does it mean? (He calls softly in a frightened voice.) Nille! Nille! Nille!--I think I'm in heaven--Nille!--and I don't deserve to be a bit. But is this myself? I think it is, and then I think it isn't. When I feel my back, which is still sore from the last beating I got, when I hear myself speak, when I stick my tongue in my hollow tooth, I think it is myself. But when I look at my nightcap, my shirt, and all the splendor before my eyes, when I hear the delicious music, then the devil split me if I can get it through my head that it is myself. No, it is not me, I'm a thousand times a low dog if it is. But am I not dreaming? I don't think I am. I'll try and pinch my arm; if it doesn't hurt, I'm dreaming. Yes, I feel it; I'm awake, sure enough; no one could argue that, because if I weren't awake, I couldn't... But how can I be awake, now that I come to think it over? There is no question that I am Jeppe of the Hill; I know that I'm a poor peasant, a bumpkin, a scoundrel, a cuckold, a hungry louse, a maggot, a lump of carrion; then how can I be an emperor and lord of a castle? No, it's nothing but a dream. So I'd better be calm and wait till I wake up. [The music strikes up again and Jeppe bursts into tears.] Oh, can a man hear things like that in his sleep? It's impossible. But if it's a dream, I hope I may never wake, and if I am crazy, I hope I may never be sane again; I'd sue the doctor that cured me, and curse the man that waked me. But I'm neither dreaming nor crazy, for I can remember everything that has happened to me: I remember that my blessed father was Niels of the Hill, my grandfather Jeppe of the Hill; my wife's name is Nille; her switch is Master Eric; my sons are Hans, Christoffer, and Niels. I've got it! I know what it is; this is the other life, this is paradise, this is heaven. I must have drunk myself to death yesterday at Jacob Shoemaker's, and when I died I went straight to heaven. Death can't be as hard to go through as they make out, for I don't feel a thing. Now, perhaps the pastor is standing this very minute in the pulpit delivering a funeral sermon over me, and is saying, "So ended Jeppe of the Hill. He lived like a soldier, and he died like a soldier." There might be some doubt as to whether I died on land or on sea, for I was easily half-seas-over when I left the world. Oh, Jeppe! how different this is from walking four leagues to town for soap, lying on straw, being beaten by your wife, and having horns put on you by the deacon. Oh, to what delights are your troubles and your bitter days now turned! Oh, I'm ready to weep for joy, particularly when I think how all this has happened to me without my deserving it! But one thing bothers me, and that is that I'm so thirsty that my lips are sticking together. If I wanted to be alive again, it would be just so I could get a mug of ale to quench my thirst, for what good is all this finery to my eyes and ears, if I'm going to die all over again of thirst? I remember, the priest often said that man neither hungers nor thirsts in heaven, and also that a man finds all his friends there. But I'm ready to faint with thirst, and I'm all alone--I don't see a soul: I should at least find my grandfather, who was such a fine man that he didn't owe his lordship a penny when he died. I'm sure lots of people have lived as good lives as I have; so why should I be the only one to go to heaven? Then it can't be heaven. But what can it be? I'm not asleep, I'm not awake, I'm not dead, I'm not alive, I'm not crazy, I'm not sane, I am Jeppe of the Hill, I'm not Jeppe of the Hill, I'm poor, I'm rich, I'm a miserable peasant, I'm an emperor. O--o--o--! Help! Help! Help! (He roars loudly.)

SCENE 2

(Enter the Valet, Eric, and others who have been watching his behavior from the doorway.)

VALET. I wish his lordship a very good morning. Here is the dressing-gown, if his lordship wishes to rise. Eric! run for the towel and basin.

JEPPE. Oh, worthy chamberlain! I will gladly get up, but I beg of you, don't hurt me.

VALET. God forbid that we should harm his lordship!

JEPPE. Oh, before you kill me, would you do me the kindness of telling me who I am?

VALET. Does not your lordship know who he is?

JEPPE. Yesterday I was Jeppe of the Hill, but to-day--Oh, I don't know what to say.

VALET. We are glad that his lordship is in such good humor to-day as to deign to jest. But, God help us, why does my lord weep?

JEPPE. I'm not your lordship. I can take my oath on it, for, as far as I can remember, I am Jeppe Nielsen of the Hill, and one of the baron's peasants. If you will send for my wife, she'll bear witness to it, but don't let her bring Master Eric along.

ERIC. This is strange. What is the matter? Perhaps my lord is not awake, for he is not accustomed to joke like this.

JEPPE. Whether I am awake or not, I can't say, but I do know and can say that I am one of my lord's peasants, who is called Jeppe of the Hill, and I never have been a baron nor a count in all my life.

VALET. Eric! what can this mean? I am afraid my lord has been taken ill.

ERIC. I imagine he is walking in his sleep, for it often happens that people get out of bed, dress, talk, eat, and drink--all while they are still asleep.

VALET. No, Eric! I think that his lordship is having hallucinations brought on by an illness, run quickly and fetch some doctors. (Exit Eric.) Oh, my lord, pray drive such thoughts from your head. His lordship will otherwise strike fear into the whole household. Does not my lord know me?

JEPPE. I don't even know myself, so how should I know you?

VALET. Is it possible that I should hear such words from my gracious lord's mouth and see him in such a plight! Alas, our unlucky house, to be plagued with an evil spell! Does not my lord remember what he did yesterday, when he went out hunting?

JEPPE. I have never done any hunting or poaching, for I know that's a thing that will get a man hard labor; no living soul can prove that I ever hunted as much as a hare in my lord's woods.

VALET. Why, my gracious lord, I was out hunting with you myself yesterday.

JEPPE. Yesterday I was at Jacob Shoemaker's, and I drank twelve pennyworth of brandy, so how could I have been hunting?

VALET. Oh, I beg his gracious lordship on my bare knees to stop talking such nonsense. Eric! have the doctors been sent for?

ERIC. Yes, they are coming immediately.

VALET. Then let us put on his lordship's dressing-gown, for perhaps he might feel better if we took him out into the open air. Will my lord be so good as to put on his dressing-gown?

JEPPE. With all my heart. You may do what you like with me, so long as you don't kill me, for I am as innocent as a babe unborn.

SCENE 3

(Enter Eric with two Doctors.)

FIRST DOCTOR. We hear with the greatest sorrow that his lordship is indisposed.

VALET. Yes, Doctor. He is in a serious condition.

SECOND DOCTOR. How are you feeling, gracious lord?

JEPPE. Splendidly, except that I'm a little thirsty from the brandy I drank at Jacob Shoemaker's yesterday. If some one would only give me a mug of ale and let me go, why then they might hang you and all the rest of the doctors, for I need no medicine.

FIRST DOCTOR. I call that pure hallucination, my good colleague!

SECOND DOCTOR. The more violent it is, the quicker it will spend its rage. Let us feel your lordship's pulse. Quid tibi videtur, Domine Frater?

FIRST DOCTOR. I think he should be bled immediately.

SECOND DOCTOR. I do not agree with you; such remarkable weakness must be treated otherwise. My lord has had a strange and forbidding dream, which has caused a commotion in his blood and has set his brain in such a whirl that he imagines himself to be a peasant. We must endeavor to divert his lordship with those things in which he usually takes the greatest pleasure. Give him the wines and the dishes that he likes best, and play the music that it pleases him most to hear. (Cheerful music strikes up.)

VALET. Is not this my lord's favorite piece?

JEPPE. Like enough. Is there always such merrymaking here in the manor?

VALET. Whenever his lordship pleases, for he gives us all our board and wages.

JEPPE. But it is strange I can't remember the things I have done before.

SECOND DOCTOR. It is the result of this illness, your lordship, that one forgets all he has done previous to it. I remember, a few years ago, one of my neighbors became so confused after drinking heavily that for two days he thought he had no head.

JEPPE. I wish Squire Christoffer would do that; he must have an illness that works just the other way, for he thinks he has a great big head, while he really hasn't got one at all, as any one can tell from his decisions. (All laugh.)

SECOND DOCTOR. It is a great pleasure to us to hear his lordship jest. But to return to my story, this fellow went all over the town asking people if they had found the head he had lost; he recovered, however, and is now a sexton in Jutland.

JEPPE. He could be that even if he hadn't found his head. (All laugh again.)

FIRST DOCTOR. Does my honored colleague remember the case that occurred ten years ago, of the man who thought his head was full of flies? He could not get over the notion, no matter how much they argued with him, until a clever doctor cured him in this way: he put on his head a plaster which was covered with dead flies, and after a while took it off and showed the flies on it to the patient, who thought they had been drawn out of his head, and was immediately well again.

I also have heard of another man who, after a long fever, got the idea that if he made water the country would suffer from a flood. No one could make him think otherwise; he said he was willing to die for the common good. This is how he was cured: a message was sent to him, supposedly from the commandant, saying that the town was threatened with a siege and there was no water in the moat, and asking him to fill it to keep the enemy out. The patient was delighted to be able to save both his fatherland and himself; so he got rid of his water and of his sickness both at once.

SECOND DOCTOR. I recall another case that occurred in Germany. A nobleman came to an inn, and when he had dined and wanted to go to bed, he hung the gold chain which he wore round his neck on a nail in the wall of the bedroom. The innkeeper took careful note of this as he followed him to bed and wished him good-night. When he thought that the nobleman was asleep, he stole into the room, cut sixty links out of the chain, and hung it up again. The guest got up in the morning, had his horse saddled, and put on his clothes. But when he came to put on the chain, he noticed that it had lost half its length, and began to call out that he had been robbed. The host, who was watching outside the door, ran in, putting on an expression of the greatest consternation, and exclaimed, "Oh, what a terrible transformation!" When the guest asked him what he meant by that, he said, "Alas, my lord! your head is as big again as it was yesterday." Then the host brought him a distorting mirror, which made everything appear twice as big as it really was. When the nobleman saw how big his head looked in the mirror, he burst into tears and said, "Oh, now I see why my chain will not go on!" Whereupon he mounted his horse, wrapping his head in his cloak, that none might see it on the road. They say that he kept the house for several days, unable to get over the idea that it was not the chain that had grown too short, but his head that had grown too big.

FIRST DOCTOR. There are countless examples of such illusions. I also remember hearing of a man who imagined his nose was ten feet long, and warned every one he met not to come too near.

SECOND FATHER. Domine Frater has undoubtedly heard the story of the man who thought he was dead? A young person got it into his head that he was dead, and consequently laid himself out on a bier, and would neither eat nor drink. His friends endeavored to show him the absurdity of his conduct and tried every means of making him eat, but in vain, for he merely dismissed them with scorn, asserting that it was contrary to all rule for the dead to eat and drink. At last an experienced physician undertook to cure him by this unusual method: He got a servant to pretend that he too was dead, and had him laid out in the same place with the patient. For a long time the two lay and looked at each other. After a while the patient began to ask the other man what he was doing there, and he answered that he was dead. Then they began to question each other as to how they had died, and both explained in full. Later, some people who had been instructed what to do came and brought the second man his supper, whereupon he sat up in his coffin and ate a hearty meal, saying to the other, "Aren't you going to eat pretty soon?" The sick man pondered over this, and asked if it was proper for a dead man to eat, and was answered that if he did not eat soon, he could not stay dead very long. He therefore allowed himself to be persuaded first to eat with the other man, subsequently to sleep, get up, dress,--in fact, in all matters copy the other, until finally he came to life and regained his senses.

I could give innumerable other examples of such odd illusions. That is just what has happened in this case to make his gracious lordship think that he is a poor peasant. But if my lord will get the notion out of his head, he will speedily be himself again.

JEPPE. But can it be only illusion?

FIRST DOCTOR. Certainly; my lord has heard from these stories what illusions can do.

JEPPE. Am I not Jeppe of the Hill?

FIRST DOCTOR. Certainly not.

JEPPE. Isn't that wicked Nille my wife?

FIRST DOCTOR. By no means, for my lord is a widower.

JEPPE. Is it pure illusion that she has a switch called Master Eric?

FIRST DOCTOR. Pure illusion.

JEPPE. Isn't it true either that I was to go to town yesterday and buy soap?

FIRST DOCTOR. No.

JEPPE. Nor that I drank up the money at Jacob Shoemaker's?

VALET. Why, your lordship was with us out hunting all day yesterday.

JEPPE. Nor that I am a cuckold?

VALET. Why, her ladyship has been dead for years.

JEPPE. I'm beginning to realize my own stupidity. I won't think about the peasant any more; I see that it was a dream that led me into my delusion. It certainly is wonderful how men get such ideas.

VALET. Does my lord wish to walk in the garden for a time while we make ready his breakfast?

JEPPE. Very well; but hurry up, for I am both hungry and thirsty.

ACT III

SCENE I

(Jeppe comes in from the garden with his suite. A small table is set.)

JEPPE. Ah, ha! I see that the table is all set.

VALET. Yes, everything is ready when his lordship wishes to be seated.

(Jeppe sits down. The others stand behind his chair and laugh at his bad manners when he sticks all five fingers in the dish, belches, and blows his nose with his fingers and wipes them on his clothes.)

VALET. Will my lord order what wine he desires?

JEPPE. You know yourself what wine I usually drink in the morning.

VALET. Here is Rhine-wine, which my lord usually drinks. But if this doesn't suit his lordship's taste, he can have something else immediately.

JEPPE. That's a little too sour. Put some mead in it, and it will be all right; I am for sweet things.

VALET. Here is some port-wine, if my lord would like to taste it.

Jeppe. That's fine wine. Shout, all of you! (Each time he drinks, trumpets blow.) Hurry up, lad! another glass of pork-wine. Do you understand?--Where did you get that ring on your finger?

SECRETARY. My lord gave it to me himself.

JEPPE. I don't remember it; give it back to me. I must have been drunk when I did it. A man doesn't give away rings like that for nothing. Later on I'll look into things and see what else you've got away with. Servants ought not to get anything more than board and wages. I can swear I don't remember making you any special present; why should I? That ring must be worth more than ten rix-dollars. No, no, my good fellows! That won't do at all. You must not take advantage of your master's feebleness and drunkenness. When I'm drunk, I'm perfectly ready to give away my breeches; but when I have slept off my liquor, I take back my gifts. Otherwise I should get into trouble with Nille, my old woman. But what am I saying? I am falling back into my mad notions again and don't realize who I am. Give me another glass of pork-wine. More noise! (Trumpets.) Pay attention to what I say, lads. I want you to understand that after this, if I give anything away in the evening when I'm drunk and you don't bring it back in the morning, you will have to answer for it. When servants are given more than they can eat, they get proud and turn up their noses at the master. What wages do you get?

SECRETARY. My lord has heretofore given me two hundred rix-dollars a year.

JEPPE. The devil a two hundred you get after this! What do you do to earn two hundred rix-dollars? I myself have to slave like a beast, and be on my feet in the hay loft from morning till night, and can scarcely--See how I come back to my cursed peasant notions. Give me another glass of wine. (He drinks; trumpets blow again.) Two hundred rix-dollars! Why, that's pulling the very hide off your master. Listen, do you know what, you good lads? When I have dined, I have a good mind to hang half you fellows here on the estate. You'll find out that I am not to be trifled with in money matters.

VALET. We will give back all that we have received from his lordship.

JEPPE. Yes, yes, "his lordship" this, "his lordship" that! We get compliments and ceremonies cheap enough nowadays. You want to flatter me with "his lordship" until you've got all my money away from me and you are the lordships yourselves. Your mouths say "his lordship," but your hearts say "his foolship." You don't say what you mean, my lads. You servants are like Abner when he came and greeted Roland, saying, "Hail, brother," and so saying thrust a dagger into his heart. Take my word for it, Jeppe is no fool. (They all fall on their knees and beg for mercy.) Get up, lads! Wait till I have finished eating. Then I shall see how it works out and decide which of you deserve to be hanged and which don't. For the present I shall make merry.

SCENE 2

JEPPE. Where is my bailiff?

VALET. He is waiting outside.

JEPPE. Tell him to come in immediately.

[Enter the Bailiff in a coat with silver buttons and a sword-belt over his shoulder.]

BAILIFF. Has his lordship any orders?

JEPPE. Only that you are to be hanged.

BAILIFF. I have surely done no wrong, my lord! Why should I be hanged?

JEPPE. Are you not the bailiff?

BAILIFF. Yes, indeed, your lordship.

JEPPE. And yet you ask why you should be hanged?

BAILIFF. I have served your lordship so honestly and faithfully and have been so diligent in my office that your lordship has always praised me more than any other of his servants.

JEPPE. Indeed, you have been diligent in your office, as your solid silver buttons plainly show. What wages do you get?

BAILIFF. Fifty rix-dollars a year.

JEPPE [gets up and walks to and fro]. Fifty? You surely shall be hanged.

BAILIFF. It couldn't well be less, my lord, for a whole year's hard work.

JEPPE. That's just the reason you are to be hanged--because you only get fifty rix-dollars. You have money enough for a coat with silver buttons, frills at your wrists, and a silk queue for your hair--and all on fifty rix-dollars a year. If you didn't rob me, poor man, where else could you get it?

BAILIFF [on his knees]. Oh, gracious lord! For the sake of my unfortunate wife and innocent children, spare me!

JEPPE. Have you many children?

BAILIFF. Seven children living, my lord.

JEPPE. Ha! Ha! Seven children living! Have him hanged immediately, Sectary.

SECRETARY. Oh, gracious lord, I am no hangman.

JEPPE. If you're not, you can soon learn to be. You look fit for any trade. And when you have hanged him, I shall have you hanged yourself.

BAILIFF. Oh, gracious lord, is there no reprieve?

JEPPE [walks to and fro, sits down, drinks, and gets up again]. Half a hundred rix-dollars, a wife and seven children. If no one else will hang you, I'll do it myself. I know what sort you are, you bailiffs! I know how you have cheated me and other miserable peasants--Oh, there come those damned peasant illusions into my head again. I meant to say, that I know your games and your goings-on so well, I could be a bailiff myself if I had to. You get the cream off the milk, and your master gets dung, to speak modestly. I really think that if the world keeps on, the bailiffs will all be noblemen and the noblemen all bailiffs. When a peasant slips something into your hand or your wife's, here is what your master is told: "The poor man is willing and industrious enough, but certain misfortunes have befallen him which make it impossible for him to pay: he has a poor piece of land, his cattle have got the scab,"--or something like that,--and with such babble your master has to let himself be cheated. Take my word for it, lad! I'm not going to let myself be fooled in that way, for I'm a peasant and a peasant's son myself--see how that illusion keeps cropping up! I was about to say that I am a peasant's son myself, for Abraham and Eve, our first parents, were tillers of the soil.

SECRETARY [on his knees]. Oh, gracious lord! Pray take pity on him for the sake of his unfortunate wife; for how can she live if he is not there to feed her and the children?

JEPPE. Who says they should live either? We can string them up along with him.

SECRETARY. Oh, my lord! she is such a lovely, beautiful woman.

JEPPE. So? Perhaps you are her lover, seeing you feel so badly about her. Send her here.

SCENE 3

[Enter Bailiff's wife; she kisses Jeppe's band.]

JEPPE. Are you the bailiff's wife?

WIFE. Yes, your lordship, I am.

JEPPE [takes her by the breasts]. You are pretty. Would you like to sleep with me to-night?

WIFE. My lord has only to command, for I am his servant.

JEPPE [to the Bailiff]. Do you consent to my lying with your wife to-night?

BAILIFF. I thank his lordship for doing my humble house the honor.

JEPPE. Here! Bring her a chair; she shall eat with me. [She sits at the table, and eats and drinks with him. He becomes jealous of the Secretary.] You'll get into trouble, if you look at her like that. [Whenever he looks at the Secretary, the Secretary takes his eyes off the woman and gazes at the floor. Jeppe sings an old love-ballad as he sits at the table with her. He orders a polka to be played and dances with her, but he is so drunk that he falls down three times, and finally lies where he falls and goes to sleep.]

SCENE 4

(Enter the Baron and Eric.)

BARON. He is sound asleep. Now we have played our game, but we have nearly been made the bigger fools ourselves, for he intended to tyrannize over us, so that we must either have spoiled our trick, or else have let ourselves be mauled by the rude yokel, from whose conduct one can learn how haughty and overbearing such people become when they suddenly rise from the mire to a station of worth and honor. If I had, in an unlucky moment, impersonated a secretary myself, I might have got a thrashing, and the whole affair would have been a failure, for people would have laughed more at me than at the peasant. We had better let him sleep awhile before we put him back into his dirty farm clothes again.

ERIC. Why, my lord, he is sleeping like a log; look, I can pound him and he doesn't feel it.

BARON. Take him out, then, and complete our little comedy.

ACT IV

SCENE 1

[Jeppe is lying on a dungheap in his old peasant clothes. He wakes and calls out.]

JEPPE. Hey, Sectary, Valet, Lackeys! another glass of pork-wine! [He looks about him, rubs his eyes as before, feels his head, and finds his old broad-brimmed hat on it; rubs his eyes again, turns the hat over and over, looks at his clothes, recognizes himself again, and begins to talk.] How long was Abraham in paradise? Now, alas, I recognize everything again--my bed, my jacket, my old cuckold-hat, myself; this is different, Jeppe, from drinking pork-wine out of a gilt-edged glass, and sitting at a table with lackeys and a sectary behind my chair. Good fortune, worse luck, never lasts very long. Oh, that I, who such a short time ago was "my lord," should now find myself in such a miserable plight, with my fine bed turned into a dungheap, my gold-embroidered cap changed into my old cuckold-hat, my lackeys into pigs, and I myself from "my lord" to a wretched peasant once more! I thought when I woke up again I should find my fingers covered with gold rings, but, saving your presence, they're covered with something very different. I thought I should be calling servants to account, but now I must get my back ready for my home-coming, when I shall have to give an account of my own doings. I thought that when I woke up I should reach out and grasp a glass of pork-wine, but instead, to speak modestly, I get a handful of dung. Alas, Jeppe, your sojourn in paradise was pretty short, and your happiness came quickly to an end. But who knows that the same thing might not happen again if I were to lie down for a while? Oh, if it only would! Oh, if I could get back there again! [Lies down and goes to sleep.]

SCENE 2

[Enter Nille.]

NILLE. I wonder if anything has happened to him? What could it be? Either the devil has taken him, or, what I fear more, he's sitting at an inn drinking up the money. I was a goose to trust the drunkard with twelve pence at once. But what do I see? Isn't that himself lying there in the filth and snoring? Oh, miserable mortal that I am, to have such a beast for a husband! Your back will pay dearly for this! [She steals up to him and gives him a whack on the rump with Master Eric.]

JEPPE. Hey, hey! Help, help! What is that? Where am I? Who am I? Who is beating me? and why? Hey!

NILLE. I'll teach you what it is soon enough. [Beats him and pulls his hair.]

JEPPE. Oh, dear Nille, don't beat me any more; you don't know all that has happened to me.

NILLE. Where have you been all this time, you guzzler? Where is the soap you were to buy?

JEPPE. I couldn't get to town, Nille.

NILLE. Why not?

JEPPE. I was taken up to paradise on the way.

NILLE. To paradise! [Hits him.] To paradise. [Hits him again.] Are you going to make sport of me into the bargain?

JEPPE. O--o--o--! As true as I'm an honest man, it's so!

NILLE. What's so?

JEPPE. That I have been in paradise. [Nille repeats "in paradise," hitting him each time.] Oh, Nille, dear, don't beat me!

NILLE. Quick, confess where you've been, or I'll trounce the life out of you.

JEPPE. Oh, I'll confess, if you won't beat me any more.

NILLE. Go on, confess.

JEPPE. Swear not to beat me?

NILLE. No.

JEPPE. As true as I'm an honest man called Jeppe of the Hill, as sure as that's true, I have been in paradise and have seen things that it will stun you to hear of.

[Nille beats him again and drags him into the house by the hair.]

SCENE 3

[Enter Nille.]

NILLE. Now, then, you drunken hound! Sleep off your liquor first; then we shall have more to say about it. Such swine as you don't go to paradise! Think of it, the beast has drunk himself clean out of his wits. But if he did it at my expense, then he'll do heavy penance for it; he shan't get a thing to eat or drink for two whole days. By that time he'll get over his notions about paradise.

SCENE 4

(Enter three armed men.)

FIRST MAN. Does a man named Jeppe live here?

NILLE. Yes, he does.

FIRST MAN. Are you his wife?

NILLE. Yes, God help me, so much the worse for me.

FIRST MAN. We must go in and talk with him.

NILLE. He's dead drunk.

FIRST MAN. That makes no difference; fetch him out or the whole household will suffer.

[Nille goes in, and pushes Jeppe out so hard that he knocks over one of the men and rolls on the ground with him.]

SCENE 5

JEPPE. Now, good friends, you see what a wife I have to put up with.

FIRST MAN. You deserve no better, for you're a malefactor.

JEPPE. What have I done now?

FIRST MAN. You'll see when justice takes its course.

SCENE 6

(Enter the Judge, followed by two Lawyers. He sits down. Jeppe, his hands tied behind him, is brought to the bar. One of his captors steps forward.)

FIRST MAN. Here is a man, your honor, whom we can swear to have seen sneaking into the baron's house, where he posed as his lordship, put on his clothes, and tyrannized over the servants. As this is a piece of unheard-of impudence, we demand on behalf of his lordship that it be punished with such severity that it shall serve as an example and a warning to other evil-doers.

JUDGE. Is this accusation true? Speak out whatever you may have to say in answer to it, for we do not wish to convict any one unheard.

JEPPE. Alas, what a God-forsaken man I am! What can I say? I admit I deserve punishment, but only for the money I squandered on drink instead of buying soap with it. I also admit that I have recently been in the castle, but how I got there and how I got out again, I haven't the least idea.

FIRST LAWYER. Your honor has it on his own admission: he got drunk and in his drunkenness committed this unheard-of outrage. All that remains is to decide whether the guilt of such a gross misdeed can be held devoid of criminal intent because of intoxication. I argue that it cannot, for if it could, neither fornication nor murder could be punished, for every criminal could seek that escape and assert that he had committed his crime while intoxicated. And although he can prove that he was drunk, his case is none the stronger, for the law is: What a man does under the influence of drink he shall answer for when sober. It is well known that in a recent case of the same nature the misdeed was punished, although the criminal was led into passing himself off as a lord through his own simplicity; his ignorance and foolishness could not save him from death. The penalty is imposed purely as a warning to others. I would tell the circumstances, were it not that I fear to delay justice thereby.

SECOND LAWYER. Your honor! This story appears so remarkable to me that I cannot accept it without the testimony of several witnesses. How could a simple peasant get into his lord's house and impersonate his lordship unless he could imitate his very form and features? How could he get into the lord's bedroom, how could he put on his clothes, without any one being aware of it? No, your honor, one can plainly see that this is the outcome of a conspiracy on the part of this poor man's enemies. I hope, therefore, that he may be discharged.

JEPPE [weeping]. God bless your mouth. I have a bit of tobacco in my breeches pocket which perhaps you won't refuse; it's good enough for any honorable man to chew.

SECOND LAWYER. Keep your tobacco, Jeppe! I speak for you not in the hope of receiving gifts, but merely from Christian charity.

JEPPE. Pardon me, Master Attorney! I didn't know you folks were so honorable.

FIRST LAWYER. What my colleague advances in favor of this man's acquittal is based entirely on conjecture. The question is not whether such a thing could happen or not, because that it did happen is proved both by witnesses and by the man's own confession.

SECOND LAWYER. What a man says from fear and awe has no weight as a confession. It seems to me, therefore, that it is best to give the simple fellow time to collect his wits, then question him over again.

JUDGE. Listen, Jeppe! Be careful what you say. Do you admit the charges against you?

JEPPE. No; I will swear my most sacred oath that it's all lies that I swore to before; I haven't been outside my door for the last three days.

FIRST LAWYER. Your honor, it is my humble opinion that he should not be allowed to testify on a matter already established by witnesses, particularly inasmuch as he has already confessed his misdeed.

SECOND LAWYER. I think he should.

FIRST LAWYER. I think he should not.

SECOND LAWYER. The case is of so unusual a nature--

FIRST LAWYER. That does not affect witnesses and a confession.

JEPPE. Oh, if they would only go for each other's throats, then I could set upon the judge and give him such a beating he would forget both law and procedure.

SECOND LAWYER. But listen, worthy colleague! Although the deed is confessed, the man has deserved no punishment, for he did no murder nor robbery nor harm of any kind while on the premises.

FIRST LAWYER. That makes no difference! Intentio furandi is the same as furtum.

JEPPE. Talk Danish, you black hound! Then I can answer for myself.

FIRST LAWYER. For when a man is taken, whether he was about to steal or had already stolen, he is a thief.

JEPPE. Gracious judge! I am perfectly willing to be hanged if that attorney can be hanged alongside of me.

SECOND LAWYER. Stop talking like that, Jeppe! You are merely injuring your own case.

JEPPE. Then why don't you answer him? [Aside.] He stands like a dumb beast.

SECOND LAWYER. But wherein is proof of furandi propositum?

FIRST LAWYER. Quicunque; in aedes alienas noctu irrumpit tanquam fur aut nocturnus grassator existimandus est; atqui reus hic ita, ergo--

SECOND LAWYER. Nego majorem, quod scilicet irruperit.

FIRST LAWYER. Res manifesta est, tot legitimis testibus existantibus, ac confitente reo.

SECOND LAWYER. Quicunque; vi vel metu coactus fuerit confiteri--

FIRST LAWYER. Oh, but where is the vis? Where is the metus? That is a quibble.

SECOND LAWYER. You're the one that quibbles.

FIRST LAWYER. No honorable man shall accuse me of that.

(They grab each other by the throat, and Jeppe jumps behind them and pulls off the First Lawyer's wig.)

JUDGE. Respect for the law! Stop, I have heard enough. [Reads aloud.] Inasmuch as Jeppe of the Hill, son of Niels of the Hill, grandson of Jeppe of the same, has been proved both by legal evidence and by his own confession to have introduced himself by stealth into the Baron's castle, to have put on his clothes and maltreated his servants; he is sentenced to be put to death by poison, and when he is dead, his body to be hanged on a gallows.

JEPPE. Oh, oh, your honor! Have you no mercy?

JUDGE. None is possible. The sentence shall be carried out forthwith in the presence of the court.

JEPPE. May I have a glass of brandy first, before I drink the poison, so I can die with courage?

JUDGE. That is permissible.

JEPPE [drinks off three glasses of brandy, and falls on his knees]. Will you not have mercy?

JUDGE. No, Jeppe! It is now too late.

JEPPE. Oh, it's not too late. A judge can reverse his decision and say he judged wrong the first time. We're all merely men, so we're all likely to make mistakes.

JUDGE. No; you yourself will feel in a few minutes that it is too late, for you have already drunk the poison in the brandy.

JEPPE. Alas, what an unfortunate man I am! Have I taken the poison already? Oh, farewell, Nille! But the beast doesn't deserve that I should take leave of her. Farewell, Jens, Niels, and Christoffer! Farewell, my daughter Marthe! Farewell, apple of my eye! I know I am your father because you were born before that deacon came around, and you take after me so we're like as two drops of water. Farewell, my piebald horse, and thank you for all the times I have ridden you; next to my own children I never loved any animal as I love you. Farewell, Feierfax, my good watchdog! Farewell, Moens, my black cat! Farewell, my oxen, my sheep, my pigs, and thank you for your good company and for every day I have known you!... Farewell,... Oh, now

I can say no more, I feel so heavy and so weak. [He falls, and lies on the floor.]

JUDGE. That worked well; the sleeping-potion has already taken effect, and he is sleeping like a log. Hang him up now, but be careful not to hurt him, and see that the rope goes only under his arms. Then we shall see what he does when he wakes up and finds himself hanging.

[They drag him out.

ACT V

SCENE 1

(Jeppe is discovered hanging from a gallows. The Judge stands aside, unseen by Nille.)

NILLE. Oh, oh, can it be that I see my good husband hanging on the gallows? Oh, my dearest husband! Forgive me all the wrong I have done you. Oh, now my conscience is roused; now I repent, but too late, for the ill nature I showed you; now that I miss you, for the first time I can realize what a good husband I have lost. Oh, that I could only save you from death with my own life's blood.

[She wipes her eyes, and weeps bitterly. Meanwhile the effects of the sleeping-potion have worn off, and Jeppe wakes. He sees that be is hanging on the gallows, and that his hands are tied behind him, and he hears his wife's laments.]

JEPPE. Be calm, my dear wife, we must all go the same way. Go home and look after the house and take good care of my children. You can have my red jacket made over for little Christoffer, and what's left will do for a cap for Marthe. Above all, see to it that my piebald horse is well cared for, for I loved that beast as if he had been my own brother. If I weren't dead, I'd have more to say to you.

NILLE. O--o--o--! What is that? What do I hear? Can a dead man talk?

JEPPE. Don't be afraid, Nille, I shan't hurt you.

NILLE. But, my dearest husband, how can you talk when you're dead?

JEPPE. I don't know myself how it happens. But listen, my dear wife! Run like wildfire and bring me eightpence worth of brandy, for I am thirstier now than I ever was when I was alive.

NILLE. Shame, you beast! You scoundrel! You hopeless drunkard! Haven't you drunk enough brandy in your living lifetime? Are you still thirsty, you sot, now that you are dead? I call that being a full-blown hog.

JEPPE. Shut your mouth, you scum of the earth! and run for the brandy. If you don't, devil take me if I don't haunt you in the house every night. You shall soon find out that I am not afraid of Master Eric any more, for now I can't feel a beating.

[Nille runs home after Master Eric, comes out again, and beats him as be hangs.]

JEPPE. Ow, ow, ow! Stop it, Nille, stop! You'll kill me all over again. Ow! ow! ow!

THE JUDGE [coming forward]. Listen, my good woman! You must not beat him any more. Be reassured; for your sake we will pardon your husband's transgression, and furthermore sentence him back to life again.

NILLE. No, no, good sir! Let him hang, for he's not worth letting live.

JUDGE. Fie, you are a wicked woman; away with you, or we shall have you hanged alongside of him.

[Nille runs away.

SCENE 2

(Enter the Judge's servants, who take Jeppe down from the gallows.)

JEPPE. Oh, kind judge, am I surely all alive again, or am I spooking?

JUDGE. You are quite alive, for the law that can take away a man's life can also give it back again. Can you not comprehend that?

JEPPE. No, indeed, I can't get it through my head, but I keep on thinking I'm a ghost, and am spooking.

JUDGE. Foolish fellow! It's perfectly easy to understand. He who takes a thing away from you can give it back again.

JEPPE. Then may I try it and hang the judge just for fun to see if I can sentence him back to life again?

JUDGE. No, that won't work, because you're not a judge.

JEPPE. But am I really alive again?

JUDGE. Yes, you are.

JEPPE. Then I'm not just a spook?

JUDGE. Certainly not.

JEPPE. I'm not a ghost at all?

JUDGE. No.

JEPPE. Am I the same Jeppe of the Hill as I was before?

JUDGE. Yes.

JEPPE. I'm no mere spirit?

JUDGE. No, certainly not.

JEPPE. Will you give me your oath that's true?

JUDGE. Yes, I swear to it; you're alive.

JEPPE. Swear that the devil may split you if it's not so. JUDGE. Come, take our word for it, and thank us for so graciously sentencing you back to life again.

JEPPE. If you hadn't hanged me yourselves, I would gladly thank you for taking me down from the gallows.

JUDGE. Be satisfied, Jeppe! Tell us if your good wife beats you too often, and we shall find a remedy. Here are four rix-dollars with which you can make merry for a while, and don't forget to drink our health.

[Jeppe kisses his hand and thanks him.]

[Exit Judge, followed by his servants.

SCENE 3

JEPPE. Now I've lived half a hundred years, but in all that time I haven't had so much happen to me as in these two days. It is a devil of a story, now that I come to think of it: one hour a drunken peasant, the next a baron, then another hour a peasant again; now dead, now alive on a gallows, which is the most wonderful of all. Perhaps it is that when they hang living people they die, and when they hang dead people they come to life again. It seems to me that, after all, a glass of brandy would taste magnificent. Hey, Jacob Shoemaker! Come out here!

SCENE 4

[Enter Jacob Shoemaker.]

JACOB. Welcome back from town! Did you get the soap for your wife?

JEPPE. You scoundrel! You shall soon find out what sort of people you're talking to. Take off your cap, for you're no more than carrion compared to the likes of me.

JACOB. I wouldn't stand such words from any one else, Jeppe, but as you bring the house a good penny a day, I don't mind it so much.

JEPPE. Take off your cap, I say, you cobbler!

JACOB. What's happened to you on the way to make you so lofty?

JEPPE. I would have you know that I've been hanged since I saw you last.

JACOB. There's nothing so splendid about that. I don't grudge you your luck. But listen, Jeppe: where you drink your liquor, there you pour out the dregs; you have gone and got full somewhere else, and now you come here to do your brawling.

JEPPE. Quick, take off your cap, scoundrel! Don't you hear what jingles in my pocket?

JACOB (his cap under his arm). Heavens, man, where did you get the money?

JEPPE. From my barony, Jacob. I will tell you all that's happened to me; but get me a glass of mead, for I'm much too high and mighty to drink Danish brandy.

JACOB. Your health, Jeppe!

JEPPE. Now I shall tell you all that's happened to me: When I left you, I fell asleep. When I woke up, I was a baron, and got drunk all over again on pork-wine. I woke up on a dungheap and went to sleep again, hoping to sleep myself back to my baron's estate. I found it doesn't always work, for my wife woke me up again with Master Eric and pulled me home by the hair, not showing the least respect for the kind of man I had been. When I got back to my room, I was thrown out again by the neck, and found myself in the midst of a lot of constables, who sentenced me to death and killed me with poison. When I was dead, I was hanged; and when I was hanged, I came to life again; and when I came to life again, I got four rix-dollars. That is my story, but as to how it happened, I leave that to you to think out.

JACOB. Ha, ha, ha! It's all a dream, Jeppe!

JEPPE. If it weren't for my four rix-dollars here, I might think it was a dream, too. Give me another, Jacob! I shan't think about all that rubbish any more, but get myself decently drunk.

JACOB. Your health, my lord baron! Ha, ha, ha!

JEPPE. Perhaps you can't grasp it, Jacob?

JACOB. No, not if I stood on my head.

JEPPE. It can be true for all that, Jacob! For you're a dunce, and there are simpler things than this that you can't understand.

SCENE 5

[Enter Magnus.]

MAGNUS. Ha, ha, ha! I'll tell you the damn'dest tale, about a man called Jeppe of the Hill, who was found lying on the ground dead drunk: they changed his clothes and put him in the best bed up at the baron's castle, made him believe that he was the baron when he woke up, got him full, and laid him in his own dirty clothes back on the dungheap again, and when he came to, he thought he had been in paradise. I nearly laughed myself to death when I heard the story from the bailiff's men. By the Lord, I'd give a rix-dollar to see the fool! Ha, ha, ha!

JEPPE. What do I owe, Jacob?

JACOB. Twelvepence.

[Jeppe strokes his chin and goes out looking very shame-faced.

MAGNUS. Why is that fellow in such a hurry?

JACOB. It's the very man they played the joke on.

MGNUS. Is that possible? I must run after him. Listen, Jeppe! Just a word--How are things in the other world?

JEPPE. Let me be.

MAGNUS. Why didn't you stay longer?

JEPPE. What business is that of yours?

MAGNUS. Come, do tell us a little about the journey.

JEPPE. Let me be, I say, or there'll be a calamity coming to you.

MAGNUS. But, Jeppe, I am so anxious to know about it.

JEPPE. Jacob Shoemaker, help! Will you let this man do me violence in your house?

MAGNUS. I'm not doing you any harm, Jeppe, I'm just asking you what you saw in the other world.

JEPPE. Hey, help, help!

MAGNUS. Did you see any of my forefathers there?

JEPPE. No, your forefathers must all be in the other place, where you and all the rest of the carrion go when they die.

[Shakes himself loose and runs away.

SCENE 6, EPILOGUE

(Enter the Baron, his Secretary, Valet, and Lackeys.)

BARON. Ha, ha, ha! That experiment was worth money. I never thought it would work out so well. If you could amuse me like that more often, Eric, you would stand even better with me than you do now.

ERIC. No, my lord! I should not dare to play that kind of comedy again. For if he had beaten your lordship as he threatened, it would have turned into an ugly tragedy.

BARON. That's very true. I was afraid of that, but I was so much engrossed in keeping up the deception that I really think I should have let myself be pummelled, or even let you be hanged, Eric, as he threatened, rather than give it away. Didn't you feel the same?

ERIC. No, indeed, my lord! It would be an odd sensation, to let yourself be hanged for fun; that sort of fun would be too expensive.

BARON. Why, Eric, such things happen every day: people throw away their lives for fun in one way or another. For instance, a man has a weak nature and sees that he is ruining his life and his health by excessive drinking; yet he still keeps on maltreating his body and risks his life for an evening's enjoyment. Then, again: it often happens in Turkey that grand viziers are strangled or choked to death with a cord the very day they are made viziers, or a few days after; yet every one is eager to take the office, just so that he may be hanged with a great title. Still another instance: officers gladly risk body and soul to get a reputation for bravery, and fight duels about anything at all even with men known to be their superiors. I think, too, that one could find hundreds and hundreds of men in love who for the sake of a night of pleasure would let themselves be killed in the morning. And you see in sieges how soldiers will desert in droves and flock to the beleaguered city, which they know must shortly surrender, and in order to live in luxury for one day will get themselves hanged the next. One way is no more rational than the other. In olden times even philosophers used to subject themselves deliberately to misfortune in order that after their death they might be praised. Therefore, Eric, I thoroughly believe that you would rather have allowed yourself to be hanged than have spoiled our beautiful practical joke.

EPILOGUE

(Spoken by the Baron)

Of this adventure, children, the moral is quite clear: To elevate the lowly above their proper sphere Involves no less a peril than rashly tumbling down The great who rise to power by deeds of just renown. Permit the base-born yokel untutored sway to urge, The sceptre of dominion as soon becomes a scourge. Let once despotic power drive justice from the realm, In every peaceful hamlet a Nero grasps the helm. Could Phalaris or Caius in days of yore have been More merciless a tyrant than him we here have seen? Before the seat of justice had time his warmth to feel He threatened us with torture, the gallows, and the wheel. Nay, never shall we tremble beneath a boor's dictates Or set a plowman over us, as oft in ancient states--For if we sought to pattern us on follies such as those, Each history of dominion in tyranny would close.

THE POLITICAL TINKER
[DEN POLITISKE KANDESTOBER]
A COMEDY IN FIVE ACTS
1722-1731

DRAMATIS PERSONAE

HERMAN VON BREMEN, a tinker.
GESKE, his wife.
ENGELKE, his daughter.

HENRICH }
ANNEKE }- his servants.
PEITER }

ANTONIUS, Engelke's lover.

JENS, a tavern-keeper }
RICHARD, a brushmaker } Members of the
GERT, a furrier }- Collegium Politicum.
SIVERT, a baggage inspector }
FRANZ, a cutler }

ABRAHAMS }
SANDERUS }- Practical jokers.

MADAME ABRAHAMS.
MADAME SANDERUS.
ARIANKE, a blacksmith's wife.

A Man pretending to be Alderman of the Hatters' Guild, Petitioners, Women, Boys, Lackeys, and others.

ACTS I and III

SCENE: Hamburg. A street, showing Herman's house.

ACTS II, IV, and V

A room in Herman's house.

ACT I

SCENE I

(A Street in front of Herman von Bremen's house. Antonius is standing before the door.)

ANTONIUS. I swear my heart's in my mouth, for I've got to talk to Master Herman and ask him for his daughter, to whom I've been engaged for ever so long, but secretly. This is the third start I have made, but each time I have turned back again. If it were not for the disgrace of it, and the reproaches I should have to take from my mother, it would be the same story over again. This bashfulness of mine is an inborn weakness, and it's not easy to get the better of it. Each time I go to knock on the door, it is as if some one were holding back my hand. But courage, Antonius, is half the battle! There is no help for it, you must go on. I should spruce myself up a bit first, for they say Master Herman is getting finicky of late. (He takes off his neck-band and ties it on again, takes a comb from his pocket and combs his hair, and dusts his shoes.) Now, I think I will do. This is the moment to knock. See! as sure as I'm an honest man, it's just as if someone were holding back my hand. Come, courage, Antonius! I know that you haven't done anything wrong. The worst that can happen to you is a "no." (He knocks.)

SCENE 2

Enter Henrich, eating a sandwich.

HENRICH. Your servant, Master Antonius. Whom do you want to see?

ANTONIUS. I wanted to talk with Master Herman, if he was alone.

HENRICH. Oh, yes, certainly he is alone. He is at his reading.

ANTONIUS. Then he is more God-fearing than I am.

HENRICH. If an ordinance were issued decreeing that the Herculus should count as a book of sermons, I believe he could qualify as a preacher.

ANTONIUS. Then has he time to spare from his work for reading such books as that?

HENRICH. You must realize that the master has two professions: he is both tinker and politician.

ANTONIUS. The two don't seem to go together very well.

HENRICH. The same idea has occurred to us. For when he does a piece of work, which is rarely, there is such a political look to the job that we have to do it all over again. But if you want to talk to him, go right into the sitting-room.

ANTONIUS. I have an important errand, Henrich, for between you and me, I want to ask him for his daughter, whom I've been engaged to for a long time.

HENRICH. My word, that is an important errand, indeed. But listen, Master Antonius, you must not take it amiss if I warn you of just one thing: if you want your suit to prosper, you must tune up your language and make a graceful speech, for he has become devilish particular recently.

ANTONIUS. No, I can't do that, Henrich! I'm a good workman, and I've never learned to pass compliments. I can only speak out straight and plain that I love his daughter and want her for my wife.

HENRICH. Nothing more? Then I'll risk my neck that you don't get her. At the very least you must start with "Whereas" or "Inasmuch." You must realize, Master Antonius, that you have to do with a learned man, who spends his days and nights in reading political works, till he's on the verge of madness. The one thing that he's found fault with lately about the people in the house is that we have such vulgar ways with us all, and myself especially--he never mentions me without calling me "You low, dirty rascal." A week or so ago he swore by the devil that Mother Geske should wear an Adrienne; still, he didn't make any headway, because mistress is an old-fashioned God-fearing woman, who had rather lay down her life than part with her lapelled bodice. He is always about to bring forth something or other, the devil knows what. So if you wish to succeed in your wooing, you had better take my advice.

ANTONIUS. Well, on my word, I don't believe in beating about the bush. I go straight to the point. [Exit into house.

SCENE 3

HENRICH. The greatest difficulty about proposing is to hit on something to start off with. I went courting once myself, but for two weeks I couldn't make up my mind what to say. I knew, of course, that you ought to begin with "Whereas" or "Inasmuch," but the trouble was that I couldn't pick out the next word to hitch on to that "Whereas." So I didn't bother about it any longer, but went and bought a formula for eightpence from Jacob tke schoolmaster--he sells them for that. But it all went wrong with me, for when I got into the middle of my speech I couldn't remember the rest of it, and I was ashamed to pull the paper out of my pocket. I swear I could recite the thing both before and afterwards like my paternoster; yet when I came to use it I stuck fast. It went like this:

"With humble wishes for your good health, I, Henrich Andersen, have come here deliberately of my own free will and on my own initiative to inform you that I am no more of a stock and a stone than others, and inasmuch as every creature on earth, even the dumb brute, is subject to love, I, unworthy as I am, have come in the name of God and Honor to beg and urge you to be the darling of my heart--" (To the audience) If any one will pay me back my eightpence, I will turn the thing over to him, for I believe that any one who made such a speech could get any good man's daughter that he had a mind to. Will you give me sixpence, then? Honestly, I paid eightpence for it myself. I'm damned if I sell it for less. But here comes the old man. I must be off. [Exit.

SCENE 4

Enter Herman and Antonius.

HERMAN. Many thanks, Monsieur Antonius, for your kind offer. You are a fine worthy fellow. I feel sure that you could take good care of my daughter. But I should very much like to have a son-in-law who had studied his politics.

ANTONIUS. But, my dear Monsieur Herman von Bremen, no one can support a wife and family on that!

HERMAN. You think not? Do you suppose I intend to die a tinker? Yon shall see, before half a year is over. I hope, when I have read through The European Herald, that I shall be urged to take a place in the council. I have already got The Political Dessert at my fingers' ends, but that is not enough. Confound the author! He might have spun it out a little. You know the book, of course?

ANTONIUS. No, not I.

HERMAN. Then I will lend you my copy. It is as good as it is brief. I have learned all my statecraft from that book, together with the Herculus and the Herculiscus.

ANTONIUS. That last one--isn't that just a romance?

HERMAN. Indeed it is, and I wish the world were full of such romances. I was at a certain place yesterday, and a man of the foremost rank whispered in my ear: "Any one who has read that book with understanding may fill the most important posts, ay, rule a whole nation."

ANTONIUS. Very good, master, but when I take to reading, I neglect my trade.

HERMAN. I tell you, monsieur, that I do not expect to confine myself to tinkering forever. I should have abandoned it long since, for hundreds of fine men here in town have said to me, "Herman von Bremen, you ought to be something else." It was only the other day that one of the burgomasters let fall these words in the council: "Herman von Bremen could surely be something more than a tinker. That man has stuff in him that many of us in the council itself might be glad to own." From which you may conclude that I shall not die a tinker. And therefore I wish to have a son-in-law who will apply himself to affairs of state, for I hope that in time both he and I shall become members of the council. And now, if you will start in with The Political Dessert, I shall examine you every Saturday evening and see what progress you make.

ANTONIUS. No, indeed, I will not. I am too old to go to school all over again.

HERMAN. Then you are not the sort to be my son-in-law. Adieu! [Exit.

SCENE 5

Enter Geske.

GESKE. It is awful about my husband; he is never at home attending to business. I would give a good deal to find out where he keeps himself. But look, here is Monsieur Antonius! Are you all alone? Won't you come in?

ANTONIUS. No, thank you, mother, I am not worthy of that.

GESKE. What nonsense is this?

ANTONIUS. Your husband has his head full of political whims, and has a burgomastership on his brain. He turns up his nose at working-people like me and my kind. He imagines that he is cleverer than the notary public himself.

GESKE. The fool! The idiot! Will you heed him? I believe he's more likely to become a vagrant and have to beg his bread, than to become a burgomaster. Dear Antonius! you mustn't pay attention to him, and you mustn't lose the affection you have for my daughter.

ANTONIUS. Von Bremen swears she shall take no one who is not a politician.

GESKE. I'll wring her neck before I see her married to a politician. In the old days they used to call a rogue a politician.

ANTONIUS. Nor do I wish to become one. I want to earn my living honestly as a wheelwright. That trade gave my honored father his daily bread, and I hope it will feed me, too. But here comes a boy who seems to be looking for you.

Enter boy.

GESKE. What do you want, my boy?

BOY. I want to talk to Master Herman.

GESKE. He's not at home. Won't you tell me?

BOY. I was to find out for my mistress, if the dish was done that she ordered three weeks ago. We have sent after it twenty times, but they always put us off with talk.

GESKE. Ask your mistress, my son, please not to be angry. It will surely be done to-morrow. [Exit Boy.

[Enter another Boy.]

SECOND BOY. I am to find out once and for all if the soup-plates will ever be finished. They could have been made and worn out since we ordered them. Mistress swore you shouldn't do any work for us again in a hurry.

GESKE. Listen, my dear child, when you order anything again, order it from me. At times my husband has bats in his belfry, and it does no good to talk to him. Believe me, on my word, it will be done by Saturday. Good-bye. (Exit Boy.) You see, my dear Antonius, how it goes in our house. We lose one job after another from my husband's neglect.

ANTONIUS. Is he never at home?

GESKE. Seldom; and when he is, he builds castles in the air so that he has no thought for work. I ask nothing of him except that he keep an eye on the workmen, for if he does anything himself, the apprentices have to do it over again. Here is Henrich: he will tell you what I say is true.

SCENE 6

(Enter Henrich.)

HENRICH. There's a man out here, mistress, who wants to be paid for the eight barrels of coal we got yesterday.

GESKE. Where can I get the money from? He will have to wait till my husband comes home. Can't you tell me where my husband is all day long?

HENRICH. If you will keep quiet about it, I can tell you right enough.

GESKE. I swear, Henrich, that I won't give you away.

HENRICH. There's a college that meets every day--Collegium Politicum, they call it--where a dozen or more people come together and chatter about affairs of state.

GESKE. Where does the meeting take place?

HENRICH. You mustn't call it a meeting, it is a Collegium.

GESKE. Where does the Collegium meet, then?

HENRICH. It meets in turn, now at one member's house, now at another's. To-day--don't tell on me--it will meet here.

GESKE. Ha, ha! Now I understand why he wants to have me out to-day calling on Arianke, the smith's wife.

HENRICH. You might go out, but come back in an hour and surprise them. Yesterday this Collegium of theirs met at Jens the tavern-keeper's. I saw them all there sitting at a table, and the master at the head of it.

GESKE. Did you know any of them?

HENRICH. I should say I did--all of them. Let me see: master and the tavern-keeper makes two, and Franz the cutler, three; Christopher the painter, four; Gilbert the paper-hanger, five; Christian the dyer, six; Gert the furrier, seven; Henning the brewer, eight; Sivert the baggage inspector, nine; Niels the clerk, ten; David the schoolmaster, eleven; and Richard the brushmaker, twelve.

ANTONIUS. They are fine fellows to discuss affairs of state! Didn't you hear what they talked about?

HENRICH. I heard well enough, but I understood very little. I heard them depose emperors and kings and electors, and set up others in their places. Then they talked about excise and consumption, about the stupid people who were in the council, and about the development of Hamburg and the promotion of trade; they looked things up in books and traced things out on maps. Richard the brushmaker sat with a toothpick in his hand; so I think he must be the secretary of their council.

ANTONIUS. Ha, ha, ha! The first time I see him I shall certainly say, "Good-day, Mr. Secretary!"

HENRICH. Yes, but don't you give me away. To the devil with fellows who put down kings and princes and even burgomaster and council!

GESKE. Does my husband join in the talk, too?

HENRICH. Not much. He just sits and ponders and takes snuff while the others talk, and when they have talked it all out, he gives his decision.

GESKE. Didn't he see you there?

HENRICH. He didn't see me because I was in another room, but if he had, his dignity wouldn't have allowed him to recognize me, for he had the air of a colonel, or of the first burgomaster when he gives audience to a minister. As soon as people get into colleges they gather a sort of mist before their eyes, and they can't see even their best friends.

GESKE. Oh, unfortunate creature that I am! That husband of mine will surely get us into trouble if the burgomaster and the council find he is setting up to reform the government. The good gentlemen don't want any reform here in Hamburg. You just see if we don't have a guard in front of the house before we know it, and my poor Herman von Bremen will be dragged off to jail.

HENRICH. That may happen, like enough; for the council has never had more power than now, ever since the troops were camped in Hamburg. All the citizens together aren't powerful enough to take his part.

ANTONIUS. Nonsense! Such fellows are only to be laughed at. What can a tinker, a painter, or a maker of brushes know about statecraft? The council is more likely to be amused than to be anxious about it.

GESKE. I will see if I can't surprise them. Let us go in till they come. [Exeunt.

ACT II

SCENE 1

(A Room in Herman's house. Herman and Henrich are making preparations for the meeting.)

HERMAN. Henrich, get everything ready: mugs and pipes on the table. They will be here in a minute. (Henrich sets everything in order. One by one the members of the Collegium Politicum enter and sit at the table. Herman takes the seat at the head of the table.) Welcome to you all, good sirs. Where did we leave off last time?

RICHARD. I think it was the interests of Germany.

GERT. That is right. I remember now. That will all be decided at the next session of the Reichstag. I wish I might be there for an hour: I should whisper something into the ear of the Elector of Mainz that he would thank me for. Those good people do not understand on what the interests of Germany depend. Where has one ever heard of an imperial capital like Vienna without a fleet or, at the very least, galleys? They could just as well maintain a war-fleet for the defence of the kingdom. There are surely war-taxes enough, and imperial subsidies. See how much more shrewd the Turk is. We can never learn to make war from any one better than from him. There are certainly plenty of forests both in Austria and in Prague, if one only will use them, to make ships, or masts, for that matter. If we had a fleet in Austria, or in Prague, the Turks and the French would give up besieging Vienna, you may be sure, and we could go straight to Constantinople. But no one thinks of such a thing.

SIVERT. No, never a mother's soul of them. Our forefathers had more sense. It is all a question of preparation. Germany is no bigger now than it was in the old days when we not only defended ourselves honorably against all our neighbors, but took in large parts of France besides, and besieged Paris by land and sea.

FRANZ. But Paris is not a seaport, is it?

SIVERT. Then I must have my map all wrong. I know well enough where Paris is. Here is England, clear enough, right where I have my finger; here flows the Channel; here is Bordeaux; and here is Paris.

FRANZ. No, brother, here is Germany, and here, right next, is France, which is joined on to Germany; ergo Paris cannot be a seaport.

SIVERT. Isn't there any seacoast to France, then?

FRANZ. Certainly not. A Frenchman who has not travelled abroad has never heard about ships and boats. Just ask Master Herman. Is it not as I say, Master Herman?

HERMAN. I shall settle the dispute at once. Henrich, give us the map of Europe--Danckwart's map.

JENS. Here is one, but it is a bit torn.

HERMAN. That makes no difference. I know well enough where Paris is, and I only need the map to convince the others. Now, look, Sivert, here is Germany.

SIVERT. That's right. I can see that by the Danube, which is here. (As he points out the Danube he upsets a mug with his elbow, and the map is flooded.)

JENS. The Danube is flowing too strongly. (All laugh.)

HERMAN. Listen, my friends. We are talking too much about foreign affairs. Let us discuss Hamburg for a while--that subject will give us material enough. I have often pondered on the question of how it happens that we own no cities in India, but are forced to buy the wares of others. That is a matter that the burgomaster and council ought to consider.

RICHARD. Don't speak of the burgomaster and council. If we wait until they think of it, we shall wait a long time. Here in Hamburg a burgomaster is commended for nothing but holding the law-abiding burgesses in subjection.

HERMAN. I believe, my good friends, that it is not too late: for why should not the king of India trade with us as well as with the Hollanders, who have nothing to send out there but cheese and butter, which usually spoil on the way? I maintain that we should do well to send a proposal to the council to that effect. How many of us are here?

JENS. We are only six, for I don't believe the other six are coming.

HERMAN. That is enough. What is your opinion, Mr. Tavern-keeper? Let us vote.

JENS. I am entirely opposed to that plan, because such voyages take away from the city a great many good men from whom I get my daily penny.

SIVERT. I hold that we ought to consider the development of the city rather than our own interests, and that Master Herman's proposal is the most admirable that can ever be made. The more trade we have, the more the city must flourish; the more ships that come in, the better for us minor officials. But the latter is not the main reason I have for favoring this plan. The city's need and its progress are the only things that persuade me to support such a scheme.

GERT. I can by no means agree to this proposal. I advise instead the founding of a company in Greenland and on Davis Strait, for that trade is much better and more useful to the state.

FRANZ. I see that Gert's vote regards his own advantage more than the welfare of the republic; for people do not need a furrier so much on the voyages to India as on voyages to the North. For my part, I contend that India surpasses all in importance; in India you can often trade a knife, a fork, or a pair of scissors with the savages for its full weight in gold. We must contrive it so that the plan we put before the council will not smell of self-interest, or else we shall get nowhere with it.

RICHARD. I am of the same opinion as Niels the clerk.

HERMAN. You certainly vote like a brushmaker. Niels the clerk is not here. But what is the woman doing here? Good Heavens, it is my wife!

SCENE 2

(Enter Geske.)

GESKE. Is this where you are, you dawdler? It would be better if you were at work on something, or at least superintending your workmen; for we lose one job after another from your neglect.

HERMAN. Quiet, wife! You will be Madam Burgomaster before you know it. Do you think that I go out just to pass the time? Ay, I do ten times as much work as all of you in the house: the rest of you work with your hands only; I work with my brain.

GESKE. All crazy people work that way, building castles in the air just as you do, cudgelling their brains with bosh and nonsense, imagining that they are doing something of importance when it is really nothing at all.

GERT. If she were my wife, she would not talk that way more than once.

FRANZ. I see that Gert's vote regards his own advantage more than the welfare of the republic; for people do not need a furrier so much on the voyages to India as on voyages to the North. For my part, I contend that India surpasses all in importance; in India you can often trade a knife, a fork, or a pair of scissors with the savages for its full weight in gold. We must contrive it so that the plan we put before the council will not smell of self-interest, or else we shall get nowhere with it.

RICHARD. I am of the same opinion as Niels the clerk. Herman. You certainly vote like a brushmaker. Niels the clerk is not here. But what is the woman doing here? Good Heavens, it is my wife!

SCENE 3

Enter Geske.

GESKE. Is this where you are, you dawdler? It would be better if you were at work on something, or at least superintending your workmen; for we lose one job after another from your neglect.

HERMAN. Quiet, wife! You will be Madam Burgomaster before you know it. Do you think that I go out just to pass the time? Ay, I do ten times as much work as all of you in the house: the rest of you work with your hands only; I work with my brain.

GESKE. All crazy people work that way, building castles in the air just as you do, cudgelling their brains with bosh and nonsense, imagining that they are doing something of importance when it is really nothing at all.

GERT. If she were my wife, she would not talk that way more than once.

HERMAN. Ah, Gert, a statesman must pay no attention to that sort of thing. Two or three years ago I should have made my wife's back smart for such words, but since I have begun to look into works on politics, I have learned to despise such trifles. Qui nesclt simulare, nescit regnare, says an ancient statesman, who was no fool. I think his name was Agrippa, or Albertus Magnus. It is a fundamental principle of all the politics in the world; for he who cannot endure an evil speech from an angry and unreasonable woman is not fit to hold any high office. Self-control is the highest virtue and the jewel which most adorns rulers and magistrates. Therefore I maintain that no one should sit in our council here in the city until he has given proof of his self-control, and made it clear that he can take words of abuse, blows, and boxes on the ear. I am by nature quick-tempered, but I try to overcome it by study. I once read in the preface of a book called The Political Stockfish that when one is overwhelmed with anger he must count twenty, and his anger will pass.

GERT. It would do me no good to count up to a hundred.

HERMAN. Then you are good for nothing but a subordinate. Henrich, give my wife a mug of ale at the side table.

GESKE. Oh, you beast! Do you think I have come here to drink?

HERMAN. One, two, three, four, five, six, seven, eight, nine, ten, eleven, twelve, thirteen--Now, it is all over. Listen, mother, you must not speak so harshly to your husband--it sounds utterly vulgar.

GESKE. Is it aristocratic to beg? Hasn't any woman reason enough to scold when she has such a good-for-nothing for a husband--a man who neglects his house like this, and leaves his wife and children in want?

HERMAN. Henrich, give her a glass of brandy, for she has worked herself into a passion.

GESKE. Henrich, give my husband a couple of boxes on the ear, the scoundrel!

HENRICH. You must do that yourself. I decline such a commission.

GESKE. Then I take it on myself. (Boxes both his ears.)

HERMAN. One, two, three-(counts to twenty, starts to strike her, but begins counting again). Eighteen, nineteen, twenty--If I hadn't been a statesman, you would have caught it that time!

GERT. If you don't keep your wife in check, I will. Get out of here. Go! Out with you!

[Exit Geske, still scolding.

SCENE 4

GERT. I 'll teach her to keep quiet at home another time. I confess that if it is statesmanlike to let yourself be dragged about by the hair by your wife, I shall never be a statesman.

HERMAN. Oh, qui nescit simulare, nescit regnare; that is easily said, but less easily done. I admit it was a great indignity my wife did me. I believe I shall run after her yet and beat her on the street. But one, two, three, four (and so on), nineteen, twenty. Now, that's all over. Let us talk of other things.

FRANZ. The women have altogether too much to say here in Hamburg.

GERT. Yes, that is so. I have often thought of bringing forward a proposal on the subject. But it is dangerous to fall out with them. Still, the proposal has its good points.

HERMAN. What is the proposal?

GERT. It consists of several articles. First, I argue that the marriage contract should not be eternal, but should be made for a term of years, so that if a man were not content with his wife, he could make a new contract with another one. A man ought to be bound, as he is with a rented house, to give a quarter's notice before moving-day, which should be at Easter or Michaelmas. If he were satisfied, the contract could be renewed. Believe me, if such a law were passed, there wouldn't be a bad woman to be found in Hamburg. Every one of them would try to gain favor in her husband's eyes so that her contract might be renewed. Have you good men anything to say against that article? Franz, you smile so knowingly, you surely have something to say against it. Let us hear it!

FRANZ. But couldn't a woman sometimes take the opportunity to separate from a husband who either was cruel to her or was an idler and only ate and drank, and refused to work to support his wife and children? Or she might take a fancy to some one else and make it so hot for her husband that, contrary to his intention, he would let her go. I argue that worse trouble might arise from such an arrangement. There are methods enough for coercing a woman. If every one would count twenty like you, Master Herman, when he got a box on the ear, we should have a fine lot of women. My humble opinion is that the best way when a woman is unruly is for the husband to threaten to sleep alone and share no bed with her till she improves.

GERT. I couldn't stick to that. To many men that would be as much of a hardship as it would be to the woman.

FRANZ. But a man can go elsewhere.

GERT. But a woman can go elsewhere.

FRANZ. Anyhow, Gert, let us hear the other articles.

GERT. I see myself! You just want to scoff some more, Nothing is so good that no fault can be found with it.

HERMAN. Let us talk of other things. People who heard us talk would think we were holding a consistory or a divorce court. I was thinking last night, as I lay awake, how the administration in Hamburg could be best arranged so that certain families whose members are born, as it were, to be burgomasters and councillors could be excluded from the highest positions of authority and complete freedom be introduced. I figured that the burgomasters should be taken in turn, now from one trade-guild, now from another, so that all citizens might share in the government and all classes flourish. For instance, when a goldsmith was burgomaster he could look after goldsmiths' interests, and a tailor after tailors', a tinker after tinkers'; and no one should be burgomaster for more than a month, so no one trade should prosper more than another. When the government was arranged like that, we might be called a really free people.

ALL. The proposition is splendid. Master Herman, you talk like a Solomon.

FRANZ. The plan is good enough, but--

GERT. You always come in with a "but." I believe your father was a butler.

HERMAN. Let him express his opinion. What were you going to say? What does that "but" of yours mean?

FRANZ. I wonder if it might not be hard at times to get a good burgomaster from every common trade? Master Herman would do, for he is well educated. But when he is dead, where shall we find another among the tinkers fitted for such responsibility? For when the republic is brought to its knees, it is not so easy to make it over into another form as it is to make over a plate or a pot that is spoiled.

GERT. Oh, nonsense! We shall find capable men a-plenty, and among artisans, too.

HERMAN. Listen, Franz. You are still a young man and so you can't see so deep into things as the rest of us, albeit I perceive that you have a good head and in time may amount to something. I can show you, briefly, that this objection of yours has no foundation, by a consideration of ourselves alone. We are twelve men in this guild, all artisans; each one of us can surely see hundreds of mistakes which the council makes. Imagine, now, that one of us becomes burgomaster and corrects all the mistakes that we have talked about so many times and that the council cannot see. Do you suppose the city of Hamburg would lose by such a burgomaster? If you good gentlemen are so disposed, I shall make that motion.

ALL. Yes, indeed.

HERMAN. But enough of these matters. Time flies, and we have not read the newspaper yet. Henrich, let us have the latest paper.

HENRICH. Here are all the latest newspapers.

HERMAN. Give them to Richard the brushmaker, who usually does the reading.

RICHARD. It is reported from headquarters on the Rhine that recruits are expected.

HERMAN. Oh, they have reported that twelve times in succession. Skip the Rhine. I could worry myself to death when I hear of such things. What is the news from Italy?

RICHARD. From Italy it is reported that Prince Eugene has broken camp, crossed the Po, and gone past all the fortifications to surprise the enemy, who thereupon retreated four miles in the greatest haste. The Duke of Vendome laid waste and burned right and left in his own territory as he retreated.

HERMAN. Upon my soul his Excellency is struck blind. We are done for. I wouldn't give fourpence for the whole army of Italy.

GERT. I maintain that the prince did right, for that has always been my plan. Didn't I say last time, Franz, that they ought to do that?

FRANZ. I don't remember that you did.

GERT. Of course I have said so, a hundred times. For why should an army lie idle? The prince has done right. I dare maintain it against any one, whoever he be.

HERMAN. Henrich, give us a glass of brandy. I swear, gentlemen, it went black before my eyes when I heard this news read.--Your health, gentlemen!--I must admit I consider it a fatal mistake to go past all the forts.

SIVERT. On my word, I should have done the same thing if the army had been entrusted to me.

FRANZ. You will see when they make generals of baggage inspectors.

SIVERT. You have no call to sneer. I should have been as good as another.

GERT. You are right there, Sivert. The prince did well to make straight for the enemy.

HERMAN. Ah, my good Gert, you are much too self-satisfied. You still have something to learn.

GERT. But not from Franz the cutler.

(They get into a violent quarrel and talk all at once. They rise from their chairs, threaten, and shout.)

HERMAN [knocking on the table and bellowing]. Silence! Silence! Gentlemen! Let us say no more about it, and each one hold to his own opinion. Listen, gentlemen! Keep still, will you? Do you think that it was from fear that the Duke of Vendome retired and set fire to the countryside? No, the fellow has been reading the Chronicle of Alexander the Great, for that's what he did when Darius followed him, and thereby he won as great a victory as we won before Hochstadt.

JENS. It has just struck twelve by the postmaster's clock.

HERMAN. Then we must go.

[They go out disputing, and make a great noise as they continue the argument.]

ACT III

SCENE 1

(In front of Herman's house stand Abrahams and Sanderus, with Christopher and Jochum, their servants.)

ABRAHAMS. I have a story for you that will amuse the whole town. Do you know what I have arranged with three or four gentlemen here in the city?

SANDERUS. No, I don't know.

ABRAHAMS. Do you know Herman von Bremen?

SANDERUS. That must be the tinker who is such a great politician and who lives in this house.

ABRAHAMS. That's the man. I was with some of the members of the council awhile ago, and they were very angry with the fellow because he talked so boldly at the tavern about the government, and wanted to reform everything. They thought it would be worth while to set spies on him to find out just what he says, so that he could be punished as an example to others.

SANDERUS. It would be a good thing to punish such fellows, for they sit over a jug of ale and criticise kings and princes and magistrates and generals in a way that is dreadful to listen to. And it is dangerous, too, for the common people hare not the discretion to appreciate how absurd it is for a tinker, a hatter, and a maker of brushes to talk about such things, of which they know little or nothing, and settle matters that are too much for the whole council.

ABRAHAMS. That is so; for that same tinker could reform the whole Roman Empire while he patched a kettle, and play both mender of dishes and mender of diets at the same time. But I did not approve the plan of those councillors, because to arrest such a man would only start an uproar among the populace and make a person of importance out of a mere fool. My idea, then, is to play a joke on him, instead, which might have better effect.

SANDERUS. How would you go about it?

ABRAHAMS. Send him a deputation, supposedly from the council, to congratulate him on his election as burgomaster, and immediately set him some hard duty to perform. Then every one will see how miserable it will make him, and he himself will realize what a difference there is between talking about an office and doing the work of it.

SANDERUS. But what will come of it?

ABRAHAMS. The result will be that he will either run away from the city out of sheer desperation, or else humbly beg for his deposition and confess his incompetence. It is only for this purpose that I have come to you, Master Sanderus, to beg your help in putting this scheme into operation, for I know that you are skilful at that sort of thing.

SANDERUS. That can be arranged. We will play the part of the deputation ourselves, and call on him immediately.

ABRAHAMS. Here is his house. Jochum or Christopher, knock, one of you, and say that two gentlemen of the council are outside and wish to talk with Herman von Bremen. (They knock.)

SCENE 2

(Enter Herman.)

HERMAN. Whom do you wish to see?

JOCHUM. Here are two gentlemen of the council, who have the honor of waiting upon you.

HERMAN. Heavens! What's up? I look as dirty as a pig.

ABRAHAMS. Your most humble servant, honorable Burgomaster! We have been sent here by the council to congratulate you on your election to the office of burgomaster of the city; for the council, after considering your merits more than your condition and circumstances, has elected you burgomaster.

SANDERUS. The council looks upon it as unjust that so wise a man should be occupied with such base affairs and should bury his great talent in the earth.

HERMAN. Honored colleagues! Convey my respects and gratitude to the just and upright councillors and assure them of my protection. I am delighted that this idea has occurred to them, not for my own sake, but for that of the city. If I had cared for rank, I might perhaps have attained something long ago.

ABRAHAMS. Honored Burgomaster! The council and the burgesses can expect nothing but the prosperity of the city under so wise a magistrate.

SANDERUS. And for that reason they have passed over so many rich and distinguished men who have sought this high office.

HERMAN. Yes, yes. I hope that they will not regret their choice, either.

ABRAHAMS and SANDERUS. We recommend ourselves, both of us, to the favor of the honorable Burgomaster.

HERMAN. It will be a pleasure to do you some service. Pardon me for not attending you further.

SANDERUS. Oh, it would hardly be fitting for your Honor to go further.

HERMAN (calling one of the lackeys). Listen, my friend! Here is something for a pot of ale.

LACKEYS. Oh, we do not do that, your Honor.

[Exeunt Abrahams, Sanderus, and Lackeys.]

SCENE 3

HERMAN. Geske! Geske!

GESKE (off stage). I haven't time.

HERMAN. Come out here! I have something to tell you that you never dreamed of in all your life.

(Enter Geske.)

GESKE. Now, what is it?

HERMAN. Have you any coffee in the house?

GESKE. What nonsense! When did I use coffee last?

HERMAN. You will need it from now on. Within half an hour you will receive calls from the wives of all the members of the council.

GESKE. I think the man is dreaming.

HERMAN. Yes, I am dreaming, in such a way that I have dreamed us into a burgomastership

GESKE. Listen, husband, don't make me angry again!

You know what happened last time.

HERMAN. Didn't you see the two gentlemen and their lackeys who went past?

GESKE. Yes, I saw them.

HERMAN. They stopped here, and brought me word from the council that I have been made burgomaster.

GESKE. The devil you have!

HERMAN. Now, my dear wife, see that you strive hereafter to acquire more correct manners, and that you retain none of your old tinker-tricks.

GESKE. Oh, is it really true, my dear husband?

HERMAN. It is as true as I'm standing here. Before we know it, we shall have the house full of congratulators, of most-humble-servants, of I-have-the-honors, and of I-kiss-your-handers.

GESKE (on her knees). Ah, my dear husband, forgive me if I have ever done you an injustice!

HERMAN. Everything is forgiven; only try to behave more like gentlefolk, and you shall find favor with me. But where shall we get a servant in a hurry?

GESKE. We must manage to get Henrich into some of your clothes until we can buy a livery. But listen, my dear: since you have become a burgomaster, I beg of you that Gert the furrier may be punished for the wrong he did me to-day.

HERMAN. Oh, my dear wife! The burgomaster's wife must not think of avenging the injury done to the tinker's wife. Let us call in Henrich.

SCENE 4

GESKE. Henrich!

HENRICH (off stage). Hey!

(Enter Henrich.)

GESKE. Henrich! you must not answer like that after this. Don't you know what has happened to us?

HENRICH. No, I don't know.

GESKE. My husband has been made burgomaster.

HENRICH. What of?

GESKE. What of? Of Hamburg!

HENRICH. The deuce you say! That certainly is the devil's own jump for a tinker!

HERMAN. Henrich, speak with more respect. You must know that you are now the lackey of a man of prominence.

HENRICH. Lackey! Then I don't advance nearly so much!

HERMAN. You shall advance in time. You may even be a reutendiener some day. Only keep still. Your duty for a few days is to act as lackey until I can get a servant.--He can wear my brown coat, my dear, till we get a livery.

GESKE. But I am afraid it will be much too long for him.

HERMAN. Of course it is too long, but a man must help himself as best he can when he's in a hurry.

HENRICH. Good Lord! It goes down to my heels. I shall look like a Jewish priest.

HERMAN. Listen, Henrich--

HENRICH. Yes, master.

HERMAN. You rascal! Don't address me by any such title any more; from henceforth, when I call, you answer "Mr. Burgomaster!" and when any one comes to ask after me, you may say, "Burgomaster von Bremenfeld is at home."

HENRICH. Must I say that whether your Honor is at home or not?

HERMAN. What nonsense! When I am not at home, you must say, "Burgomaster von Bremenfeld is not at home;" and when I do not wish to be at home, you shall say, "The burgomaster is not giving audience to-day."--Listen, my dear, you must make some coffee immediately, so that you will have something to entertain the councillors' wives with when they come. For our reputation will from now on depend on having people say, "Burgomaster von Bremenfeld gives good counsel, and his wife good coffee." I am so much afraid, my dear, that you will make some mistake before you get accustomed to the position that you have attained.--Henrich, run get a tea-table and some cups, and tell the girl to run out and get fourpence' worth of coffee--one can always buy more later.--You make it a rule, my dear, not to talk much until you learn to carry on refined conversation. You must not be too humble, either, but stand upon your dignity, and strive in every way to get the old tinkering habits out of your head, and try to imagine that you have been a burgomaster's wife for years. In the morning a tea-table must be set for callers, and in the afternoon a coffee-table, and that can be used for cards. There is a game that they call Allumber; I would give a hundred thalers if you and our daughter, Miss Engelke, knew how to play it. You must pay close attention when you see other people play, so you can learn it. You must lie abed in the morning till nine or half past, for it's only common people who get up in the summer with the sun. But on Sunday you must get up a little earlier, as I expect to take physic on that day. You must get hold of a fine snuff-box, and let it lie on the table near you when you are playing cards. When any one drinks your health, you mustn't say "Thanks," but "Tres humble servitoor." And when you yawn, you mustn't hold your hand before your mouth, because that isn't done any more among the gentry. And lastly, when you are in company, you mustn't be too squeamish, but leave your propriety a little to one side.--Listen, I forgot something: you must also get a lap-dog and love it like your own daughter, for that's fashionable. Our neighbor Arianke has a pretty dog that she might lend you till we can get one for ourselves. You must give the dog a French name, which I shall think up when I have time. It must lie in your lap constantly, and you must kiss it at least half a dozen times, when there are callers.

GESKE. No, my dear husband, I can't possibly do that, for there's no telling what a dog has been lying in and getting itself all dirty--you might get a mouthful of filth or fleas.

HERMAN. Here, here, no nonsense! If you want to be a lady, you must act like a lady. Besides, a dog like that can supply you with conversation; when you have run short of topics, you can talk about

the dog's qualities and accomplishments. Just do as I say, my dear;
I understand high society better than you do. Take me as your model.
You shall find that not even the smallest of my old habits will
remain. It won't happen to me as it did to a butcher, once, when he
was made a councillor. Whenever he had written a page and wanted to
turn over the leaf, he put his pen in his mouth, as he used to do
with his butcher's knife. The rest of you go in now and get things
ready. I want to talk awhile with Henrich alone.

[Exit Geske.]

SCENE 5

HERMAN. Listen, Henrich!

HENRICH. Mr. Burgomaster!

HERMAN. Don't you think people will envy me because of this preferment?

HENRICH. Well, what do you care about people who envy you, your Honor? If only I had been made a burgomaster like that, I should have sent my enviers to death and the devil.

HERMAN. The one thing I am a little anxious about is the matter of small ceremonies, for the world is governed by pedantry, and people notice trifles more than solid things. If only the first day were over, when I make my entry into the City Hall, I should be glad; for as far as substantial business is concerned, that is bread and butter to me. But I must arrange how I am to meet my colleagues for the first time and make sure that I do not run counter to any of the traditional ceremonies.

HENRICH. Oh, fiddlesticks, Mr. Burgomaster! No true man lets himself be bound by fixed ceremonies. I, for my part, should do nothing, if I were to make my entry, except give the gentlemen of the council my hand to kiss, and wear a fine scowl on my brow so that they might gather what my intentions were, and silently make them realize that a burgomaster was no goose and no dumpling.

HERMAN. But think, there must be an oration at the City Hall the first day that I am introduced. I can certainly make as good a speech as any one in town, and I should make bold to preach if it were to-morrow morning. But inasmuch as I have never been present at such a ceremony before, I really don't know what is the customary formula.

HENRICH. Oh, sir, no one but schoolmasters limit themselves by a formula. If I were burgomaster, I should be content with a brief and emphatic address, such as this: "It may seem a rather remarkable thing, wise and noble councillors, to see a miserable tinker suddenly turned into a burgomaster--"

HERMAN. Fie, that would be a shabby start.

HENRICH. No, that wouldn't be the start. I should begin my speech like this: "I thank you, wise and noble gentlemen, for the honor you have done a wretched tinker like me in making him burgomaster--"

HERMAN. You always bring in your confounded "tinker." It is not proper to talk like that at the City Hall, where I must act as if I had been born a burgomaster. If I were to make such a speech, I should only be scorned and mocked. No, no, Henrich, you would make a poor orator. He is a rogue who says I was ever a tinker. I have merely tinkered a little to pass the time away when I have been tired of studying.

HENRICH. He is a rogue who says I was ever a tinker's apprentice.

HERMAN. Then why do you want me to make such a speech?

HENRICH. Oh, have a little patience! Your Honor is too hasty. I should politely tell them at the start that if any one made fun of me for having been a tinker, he would get into trouble. And if I noticed the least expression of mockery on any one's face, I should say, "Wise and noble sirs, do you for a moment allow yourselves to imagine that you have made me burgomaster to ridicule me: And at that I should pound hard on the desk while I spoke, so that they might see from my introductory speech that I was not to be fooled with, and that they had made a burgomaster who was the man for the place. For if his Honor lets himself be imposed on at the start, the council will continue to look on him as a rascal."

HERMAN. You talk like a rascal, but still I shall manage to hit on the kind of speech I want to make. Let us go in.

[Exeunt.

ACT IV

SCENE I

(A Room in Herman's house. Henrich, alone. He has braid on both sleeves of his coat, which reaches to his heels, and is trimmed with white paper.)

HENRICH. I am a cur if I can see how the council hit on the idea of making my master burgomaster, because I can see no connection between a tinker and a high official like that, unless it is that just as a tinker throws plates and dishes into a mould and melts them up into new ones, so a good burgomaster can remould the republic, when it is declining, by making good laws. But the good men did not take into consideration the fact that my master is the worst tinker in Hamburg, and therefore, if they have by any chance chosen him on that basis, he will be the worst burgomaster, too, that we have ever had. The only useful thing about their choice is that it makes me a reutendiener, and that is a position for which I have both talent and inclination, for ever since I was a boy I have enjoyed seeing people arrested. It is a good place, too, for one who knows how to make something out of it. First of all I must appear to have a great deal of say with the burgomaster, and when people get that article of faith through their heads, Henrich will make at least a hundred or two hundred thalers a year, which I shall take not out of greed, but only to show that I understand my business as reutendiener. If any one wants to talk to the burgomaster, I say he is not at home. If they say they saw him at the window, I answer that it makes no difference, he is still not at home. People in Hamburg know at once what that answer means; they slip a thaler into Henrich's hand, and his Honor promptly comes home. If he has been ill, he recovers at once; if he has had visitors, they leave at once; if he has been lying down, he gets up at once. I run about with the lackeys of the gentry, now and then, and I know well enough what goes on in those houses. In the old days when folks were as stupid as horses and asses, such things were called stealing, but now they are known as "extras," "tips," or "unclassified income." But look, here comes Anneke; she doesn't know yet about the transformation, for she still has her vulgar tinker-look and tinker-walk.

SCENE 2

[Enter Anneke.]

ANNEKE. Ha, ha, ha! He looks like a mummer. I believe that's an Adrienne that he's got on him.

HENRICH. Listen, you tinker's trash! have you never seen a livery or a lackey before? Faith, these common people are like animals, they stand and stare like cows, when they see a man in different clothes one day from what he wears another.

ANNEKE. No, a joke's one thing, and sober truth's another. Don't you know that I've learned to tell fortunes? An old woman came here to-day who reads people's hands. I gave her a bit of bread and she taught me the art of seeing in people's hands what is going to happen to them. If I may look at your hand, I can tell your fortune at once.

HENRICH. Yes, yes, Anneke! Henrich isn't as stupid as you think. I smell a rat already. You have got wind of the promotion that is promised me to-day.

ANNEKE. No, indeed, I know nothing about it.

HENRICH. See how straight she keeps her face. Indeed you have heard it, and that is why you know how to tell fortunes so well. No, Henrich has an old head on his shoulders, and he can't be led by the nose.

ANNEKE. I give you my oath that I haven't heard a word of what you are talking about.

HENRICH. Haven't you been talking to madam the burgomaster's wife?

ANNEKE. The fellow is mad. What burgomaster's wife do I know?

HENRICH. Then I believe the young lady has told you.

ANNEKE. Here, enough of this nonsense, Henrich.

HENRICH. Look here, Anneke, here is my hand. Tell my fortune all you want. I see well enough that you have got wind of the affair, although you act as if you knew nothing about it. But it can do no harm to have you so wily; our whole household must be like that from now on. Now, what do you see in my hand?

ANNEKE. I see, Henrich, that master's custos which hangs back of the stove will dance a merry step on your back this day. Aren't you ashamed to go round like a mummer when there is so much work to do in the house, and to treat the master's coat like that?

HENRICH. Listen, Anneke! I can tell fortunes without reading hands. I prophesy that you are a rascal, and for your shameless talk you are going to get a box on the ear, or two, as the case may be. See, there's a prophecy come true. (Boxes her ear.)

ANNEKE. Ow, ow, ow! You shall pay dear for that.

HENRICH. Learn to show ordinary respect another time for a great gentleman's lackey--(Boxes her ear again.)

ANNEKE. Just you wait; mistress will be here in a minute.

HENRICH (again).--for the burgomaster's most distinguished servant--

ANNEKE. She will take it out on your back.

HENRICH (again).--for a reutendiener--

ANNEKE. Yes, yes! I say it again: that will cost you dear.

HENRICH (again).--for a person of great influence with the burgomaster--

ANNEKE. Oh, oh! No one in this house has ever struck me before.

HENRICH (again).--whom all the citizens will cherish and compliment henceforth.

ANNEKE. I think the fellow is stark mad. Oh, mistress! mistress! Come here!

HENRICH. Hush, hush! You will get into trouble with your mistress. I see now that you don't know what has happened, so, like a Christian, I forgive your fault. The council has unanimously elected the master burgomaster, mistress madam burgomaster, and decreed Engelke out of mere maidenhood into the degree of young lady. Therefore you can easily understand that it won't do for me to work any more. For the same reason, too, I wear this livery that you notice.

ANNEKE. Well, don't stand and stare at me into the bargain.

HENRICH. It is as I say, Anneke! Here comes the young lady, who shall vouch for my words.

SCENE 3

(Enter Engelke.)

ENGELKE. Oh, God help me, poor creature! Now I see that all hope is gone.

HENRICH. Oh, my young lady, is this the time to weep, when your parents have come into such good fortune?

ENGELKE. Hold your tongue, Henrich, I don't want to be "my young lady."

HENRICH. What are you going to be, then? You're not a mere maiden, so you must be a young lady. That is surely the next degree of honor to which you rise when you lose your maidenhood.

ENGELKE. I had rather be a peasant's daughter. Then I could be sure of getting the man on whom I have set my heart.

HENRICH. Oh, is that all the young lady is crying about--that she wants to get married? Now she can get married in the shortest possible time to any man she points at, for half the town will besiege the house to be a burgomaster's son-in-law.

ENGELKE. I won't have any one but Antonius, whom I've already promised to marry.

HENRICH. Fie, Mamsell! Will you take a wheelwright now, a man I can scarcely associate with,--I, who am only a reutendiener? You should have a higher sense of honor after this.

ENGELKE. Be quiet, you lout! I would give up my life rather than let myself be forced to marry any one else.

HENRICH. Now reassure yourself, my young lady, we shall see, I and the burgomaster, if we can't help Antonius into office, and then you can take him and welcome. (Exit Engelke. Anneke weeps.) Why are you crying, Anneke?

ANNEKE. I am crying for joy over the fortune that has come to our house.

HENRICH. True enough, Anneke, you have cause to rejoice. Who the devil would have thought that such a sow as you are could ever become a lady's maid?

ANNEKE. And who the dickens could have thought that such a hog as you might become a reutendiener?

HENRICH. Listen, little girl, I haven't time to talk to you any longer now. Madam expects guests; I must prepare coffee. See, here she is; let us go. I must run get the coffee-table. [Exeunt.

SCENE 4

(Enter Geske with a dog in her arms. Henrich returns with the coffee-table and sets it busily.)

GESKE. Listen, Henrich, is there syrup in the coffee?

HENRICH. No, Mistress!

GESKE. No more "Master" and "Mistress," Henrich! I say that once for all. Run get some syrup and put it into the pot. (Exit Henrich.) I was free from all this hubbub before. But I suppose that once I am used to it, it will come easier to me.

(Enter Henrich.)

HENRICH. Here is the syrup.

GESKE. Pour it into the pot. Goodness me, some one is knocking. It must be the wives of councillors to call on me.

HENRICH (at the door). Whom do you want to speak to?

GIRL. Tell your master that he can lie like ten tinkers. I have worn out a pair of shoes running to and fro after the dripping-pan.

HENRICH. I say, whom do you want to speak to?

GIRL. I want to speak to Master Herman.

HENRICH. You are on a wild-goose chase. Burgomaster von Bremenfeld lives here.

GIRL. It is a scandal when people can't get their things done, and have to let themselves be made fools of by a miserable tinker.

HENRICH. If you have any fault to find with tinkers, you must go to the Council Hall; you will get justice there, or I don't know Burgomaster von Bremenfeld.

TWO LACKEYS. Our ladies are desirous of announcing that if it suits the convenience of Madam Burgomaster, they should like to have the honor of waiting on her.

HENRICH (to the Girl). Now, do you see, you scum of the earth, that it's no tinker that lives here? (To the servants.) I will inquire if the burgomaster's lady is at home.

[The Girl goes.

HENRICH (to Geske). Here are two councillors' ladies outside, who want to talk to the mistress.

GESKE. Let them in.

SCENE 5

(Enter Madame Abrahams and Madame Sanderus. They kiss Geske's apron.)

MME. ABRAHAMS. We have come here to-day to offer our most humble congratulations and to témoigner the heartfelt joy and delight that we feel at your advancement, and at the same time to recommend ourselves to your favor and affection.

GESKE. Tres humble servitoor! I wonder if you wouldn't like to drink a cup of coffee.

MME. ABRAHAMS. We thank Madam Burgomaster, but this time we have come only to offer congratulations.

GESKE. Tres humble servitoor! But I know you like coffee. Perhaps you just want to be urged. Be so good as to sit down; the coffee is all ready. Henrich!

HENRICH. Gracious madam?

GESKE. Have you put the syrup in the coffee?

HENRICH. Yes, I have. [Exit.

GESKE. Please, good ladies, won't you have some?

MME. SANDERUS. I hope you will be so good as to excuse us, but we never drink coffee.

GESKE. Oh, nonsense, I know better I beg you be seated.

MME. SANDERUS (aside to Mme. Abrahams). Oh, ma soeur, I am sick at the mere thought of that syrup.

GESKE. Henrich, come fill the cups.

(Enter Henrich.)

MME. SANDERUS. That is enough, my good man. I can drink only half a cup.

HENRICH. I am to ask Madam Burgomaster to step in for a moment and speak to the burgomaster.

GESKE. Excuse me, good ladies, I must go for an instant. You shall shortly have the honor of seeing me again.

[Exeunt Henrich and Geske.

SCENE 6

MME. ABRAHAMS. Ha, ha, ha, ha, ha, ha, ha, ha, ha! Whom is the joke on now, my sister, she whom we laugh at in our sleeves as we sit here, or we who have to drink coffee with syrup in it?

MME. SANDERUS. For Heaven's sake don't mention the syrup again! My stomach comes up into my throat when I think of it.

MME. ABRAHAMS. Did you notice the airs she put on when we kissed her apron? Ha, ha, ha, ha, ha! I shall never forget as long as I live that "Tres humble servitoor." Ha, ha, ha, ha, ha!

MME. SANDERUS. Don't laugh so loud, sister, I'm afraid they can hear it.

MME. ABRAHAMS. Oh, it is a real art to be able to keep from laughing. And wasn't that the sweetest dog she had in her arms? The loveliest watch-dog one might wish for. I am sure it was called "Joli" into the bargain. Heavens, heavens, how true it is, as people always say, that no one is more arrogant than those who come up from the dregs into positions of honor! That is why nothing is more dangerous than these sudden changes. People who are of good stock and are properly brought up are only too glad to stay as they were, or even to become more humble, when they rise to higher distinction. But those who grow up quickly out of nothing, like mushrooms, seem to come naturally by intolerable pride.

MME. SANDERUS. I wonder what the reason can be? I should think such people ought rather to be humbled by the thought of their former position.

MME. ABRAHAMS. The reason must be that those who come from good families have never suspected any one of despising them, and consequently don't worry about how they are received, whereas common people have always suspected every one, and think that every word and every glance is intended as a reflection on their previous state, and so they seek to assert their dignity by making themselves imperious and tyrannous. Believe me, dear sister! There is something in springing from good stock. But here comes the boy; we had better be still.

SCENE 7

(Enter Henrich.)

HENRICH. The good ladies must not let the time seem long. The madam is coming back in a minute. The burgomaster has presented her with a new collar for her dog, but it was a little too wide; so the tailor is in there taking the measure of the dog's neck. As soon as that's settled, she will come back. But I hope you good ladies won't take it amiss, if I ask you a favor: will you be so good as to think of me in a little remembrance, for I have heavy work, and slave like a beast here in the house.

MME. ABRAHAMS. Gladly, my friend! Here is a gulden,--you will accept it.

HENRICH. Ah, my best thanks! I hope that I may serve you ladies again. Now, you must drink your fill while the mistress is out; she won't be angry, or if she is, I will make it all right.

MME. ABRAHAMS. My good man, the greatest service you can do us is not to urge us.

HENRICH. As I say, gentle ladies, I know the mistress won't mind; you simply must drink. Perhaps it isn't sweet enough. I will go get some more syrup.--But here she comes herself.

SCENE 8

(Enter Geske.)

GESKE. I beg your pardon for staying away so long. ladies, you haven't drunk a thing in all this time! We simply must empty the pot, and then when you have the coffee, you must taste our ale. If I do say it it is as good as any ale in town.

MME. SANDERUS. Oh, I feel so very bad, you must pardon me if I am unable to stay any longer. My sister will stay and try it.

MME. ABRAHAMS. Oh, no, it would be a sin to desert my sister. We commend ourselves to the affection of Madam Burgomaster.

GESKE. Then you must have a glass of brandy--it will make you perfectly well again--it drives out the wind. Henrich! run get a glass of brandy--the lady's not feeling well.

MME. SANDERUS. No, excuse me; I must go. [Exeunt.

SCENE 9

(Enter another Councillor's Wife.)

COUNCILLOR'S WIFE. Your humble servant. I have come dutifully to extend my felicitations.

(Geske reaches out her hand to be kissed, and the lady kisses it.)

GESKE. It will be a pleasure to me if I or the burgomaster can be of any service. Won't you sit down, please? Don't stand on ceremony, just imagine that you are among your equals.

COUNCILLOR'S WIFE. I am deeply obliged, madam! (Sits down.)

GESKE. Some of your colleagues were just here and drank some coffee with me; I think there must be a couple of cups left, if you should like some. The bottom's the best. I don't believe I can drink any more, because I've got so much in me already that my stomach's like a drum.

COUNCILLOR'S WIFE. I thank you humbly, but I have just had some coffee.

GESKE. As you wish. We gentlefolk don't urge any one. Oh, listen, dear madam--do you know of any Frenchwoman to recommend for my young
lady? I want her to learn French.

COUNCILLOR'S WIFE. Yes, my lady, I know one who is very satisfactory.

GESKE. Good; but I want to have her understand at the outset that I cannot tolerate having her call me "Madame" as the French people usually do. Not that I am proud, but I have my own ideas on the point.

COUNCILLOR'S WIFE. Oh, no, of course she must not. But might I not also have the privilege of kissing your daughter's hand?

GESKE. I should be delighted. Henrich! Call the young lady and tell her that a lady of the council is here and wishes to kiss her hand.

HENRICH. I don't think she can come, because she's darning her stockings. [Exit.

GESKE. Just listen to that lout, how he stands there and talks at random! Ha, ha, ha! He means to say "embroidering."

SCENE 10

(Enter Arianke, the Blacksmith's Wife. (This part is played by a man.))

ARIANKE. Oh, my dear sister Geske! Is it true that your husband has been made burgomaster? I am as pleased as if I had been given two marks. Let us see now that you haven't become proud, but acknowledge your old cronies. (Geske does not answer?) When was your husband made burgomaster? (Geske says not a word.) You are getting absent-minded, sister. I am asking you when your husband was made burgomaster.

COUNCILLOR'S WIFE. You must show a little more respect, dear Madam, to a burgomaster's wife.

ARIANKE. No, I don't have to stand on ceremony with sister Geske, for we have been like body and soul. But what is the matter, sister? It seems to me that you have grown a bit haughty.

GESKE. My good woman, I don't know you.

ARIANKE. The Lord preserve us! When you needed money, you knew me well enough. You can't be sure but my husband may come to be the same as yours some time before he dies.

(Geske turns faint and uses a bottle of smelling-salts.)

HENRICH. Get out, you smith's hag! Do you think you're standing in a smithy and talking?

[Takes her by the hand and leads her off.]

GESKE. Oh, madam, it is a sorrow to associate with these low-born people. Henrich! you will get into trouble if you let in any more commoners' wives after this.

HENRICH. She was drunk as a pig; the brandy fairly stuck out off her throat.

COUNCILLOR'S WIFE. The incident pains me, for I fear that Madam Burgomaster has been overcome by anger. People of rank cannot endure much. The higher one advances in position, the more delicate one's health becomes.

GESKE. Yes, I can assure you that I am far from having the health now that I had in my former rank.

COUNCILLOR'S WIFE. I can believe that easily. Madam will have to take physic every day. All other burgomaster's wives have had to do it.

HENRICH (aside to the audience). I think, by Jove, that I haven't the health I used to have, since I became reutendiener. I've got a stitch--oh, oh!--right here in my left side. You laugh at it, good people, but I am really in earnest. Ma foi, I am afraid that before I know it I shall have gout on me.

COUNCILLOR'S WIFE. Madam must also engage a doctor by the year for her whole household, and he can give her some drops which she can at least leave standing in a bottle, whether she uses them or not.

GESKE. Yes, I certainly shall follow your advice. Henrich! Later on you must run to Doctor Hermelin's and ask him to make me a visit when he has time.

COUNCILLOR'S WIFE. I must now take my leave, madam, and commend myself to your affection.

GESKE. Already so commended, my dear lady! You have but to speak frankly to me or to Master Herman--I mean to Burgomaster von Bremenfeld. What service we can do to you or to those dear to you, you shall never lack.

COUNCILLOR'S WIFE (kissing her apron). Your most humble servant!

GESKE. Adieu! (Exit the Councillor's Wife.) Let us go in, for my husband is giving audience here.

ACT V
SCENE I

(Same as Act IV. Henrich, alone.)

HENRICH. Well, well, here comes grist to my mill; it's the audience hour. Now, you shall see, good people, if a man who had been twenty years in the service could bear himself better than I.--There's some one knocking. Whom do you wish to see, my good men?

(Enter two Lawyers.)

FIRST LAWYER. We should very much like to have the honor of speaking to the burgomaster.

HENRICH. He is not up yet.

FIRST LAWYER. Not up at four in the afternoon?

HENRICH. Oh, he is up, to be sure, but he has gone out.

FIRST LAWYER. But we just met a man at the door who had been talking to him.

HENRICH. He really is in, but he is not well. (Aside.) These fellows are as stupid as cattle, they don't seem to grasp my meaning.

FIRST LAWYER (aside). I perceive, mon frere, that this fellow wants to be oiled; we must slip a gulden into his fist, and then the burgomaster will come fast enough. Listen, my friend! You will not refuse a couple of gulden to drink our healths with?

HENRICH. Oh, no, my dear sirs, I never take anything as a present.

FIRST LAWYER. What shall we do, then, mon frere? Evidently we must go away until another day.

HENRICH (beckons to them). Hey, gentlemen! you are in too much of a hurry. For your sake I will accept the two guldens; otherwise you might think that I was proud and our house would be ill spoken of in consequence.

FIRST LAWYER. Here, comrade! Here are two guldens, if you will accept them; now be good enough to obtain us an audience.

HENRICH. Your most humble servant. For your sake I shall do all I can. The burgomaster is really as sound as a horse, but still he is not well enough to talk with every one. But seeing that it is you, gentlemen, it is another story. If you will be so good as to wait a moment, gentlemen, I will announce you. But there's some one else knocking. Whom do you want to see, my good man?

(Enter a Man.)

MAN (feeling in his breeches pocket). I should like to have the honor of talking with the burgomaster.

HENRICH (aside). This man knows the ropes: he goes right for his pocket. (Aloud.) Yes, sir, he is at home. You may speak to him immediately.

(Henrich reaches out his hand, but the other instead of money merely pulls out his watch.)

MAN. I see it is already four o'clock.

HENRICH. Who was it you wished to see?

MAN. The burgomaster.

HENRICH. He is not at home, sir.

MAN. You just said that he was at home.

HENRICH. Perhaps I did, sir, but if I did, I made a mistake. (Exit Man. Henrich goes on, aside.) Look at that sharper! Now you shall see if the burgomaster is at your beck and call! (To the lawyers.) I shall announce you immediately. [Exit

FIRST LAWYER. Just see how that rascal knows how to fit into his place already. Keep good countenance, mon frere, it is we who shall start the plaguing of the good tinker. Our comrades will complete the tale. But here he comes.

SCENE 2

(Enter Herman and Henrich.)

FIRST LAWYER. From the bottom of our hearts we wish the honorable Burgomaster the greatest success in his high position in our city, and hope that in gentleness, foresight, and vigilance he may not fall behind his predecessors, inasmuch as his Excellency has made his way to this high office not through wealth, family, or friends, but purely by reason of his well-known great virtues, learning, and experience in affairs of state.

HERMAN. Tres humble servitoor!

SECOND LAWYER. Especially do we rejoice that we have now an administration endowed not only with almost godlike understanding--

HERMAN. I thank God--

SECOND LAWYER.--but one who has the reputation of being friendly to all and of making it his greatest delight to hear the people's grievances and to help to right them. I may say that I almost fainted with joy when I first heard the news that the choice had fallen on Burgomaster von Bremen.

HENRICH. You must say "Bremenfeld," gentlemen.

SECOND LAWYER. I humbly beg your pardon: I should say, "Burgomaster von Bremenfeld." To-day we have come here, in the first place to extend our respectful congratulations; in the second place to consult your Magnificence on a difference that has arisen between our clients, which difference we had both agreed to have judged according to the common law of the land and the statutes. But we subsequently changed our mind and decided, in order to save time and costs, to submit ourselves to your judgment, and we promise to abide by that.

(Herman sits down, leaving the others standing.)

FIRST LAWYER. Our clients are neighbors, but there is running water separating their land. Now it happened that three years ago the water loosened a large piece of earth from my client's estate and deposited it on my opponent's field. Shall he now own it? Is it not stated: Nemo alterius damno debet locupletari? Here his client wishes to enrich himself at my client's expense, which aperte conflicts with aequitatem naturalem. Is that not so, Mr. Burgomaster?

HERMAN. Of course; it is unjust to ask that. You are right, monsieur!

SECOND LAWYER. But does not Justinian say expressly, libro secundo Institutionum, titulo prima, de Alluvione...

HERMAN. What the deuce do I care for what Justinian or Alexander the Great says? They lived a few thousand years, perhaps, before Hamburg was founded. How can they decide in cases which didn't exist in their time?

SECOND LAWYER. I hope, however, that your Honor is not going to reject the laws that all Germany has submitted to.

HERMAN. That was not the way I meant it; you misunderstood me, I only meant to say--(He has a coughing fit.) Kindly continue your case.

SECOND LAWYER. There are the words of Justinian: Quod per alluvionem agro tuo flumen adjecit, jure gentium tibi acquiritur.

HERMAN. Mr. Lawyer, you speak so devilish fast--say that over, more distinctly. (The lawyer repeats the Latin slowly.) Monsieur, you have a devilish bad Latin pronunciation. Speak your mother-tongue, and you will do better. I don't say this because I have any prejudice against Latin, for I sometimes sit and talk Latin with my servant for hours at a time. Isn't that so, Henrich?

HENRICH. It is wonderful to hear his Honor talk Latin; I swear the tears come into my eyes when I think of it. It is like listening to peas boiling in a pot, the words come so quickly from his mouth. The devil himself doesn't know how a man can manage to talk so fluently. But what won't long practice do for you?

SECOND LAWYER. Justinian's words, your Magnificence, are as follows: Whatsoever a river wears off another's field and casts up on yours, that belongs to you.

HERMAN. Yes, Justinian is right so far, for he was a fine man. I have much too much respect for him to question his decision.

FIRST LAWYER. But, your Honor, my opponent interprets law as the devil does the Bible. He forgets what follows right after: Per alluvionem autem videtur id adjici, quod ita paulatim adjicitur, ut intellegere non possis, quantum quoquo temporis momenta adjiciatur.

HERMAN. Messieurs! I must go to the City Hall. The clock has just struck half-past four. Henrich! See to it that you adjust this suit in the entry.

FIRST LAWYER. Ah, your Honor! Give us your opinion in a word.

HERMAN. Messieurs, you are both right, each one in his own way.

SECOND LAWYER. How can we both be right? I maintain that if I am right, my antagonist is wrong. The law of Justinian is expressly in my favor.

HERMAN. Excuse me, I must be off to the City Hall immediately.

FIRST LAWYER (seizing hold of him). I have certainly proved that Justinian's opinion is on my side.

HERMAN. Yes, that is so. Justinian is for both of you. Why the devil, then, don't you compromise? You don't know Justinian as well as I do; when he wears the mantle on both shoulders, it is as much as to say: Get out, you scurvy-necks, and compromise!

SECOND LAWYER. Your Honor, in order to grasp the jurist's meaning correctly, one must compare one article with another. Is it not written in the very next paragraph: Quodsi vis fluminis de tuo praedio--?

HERMAN. Here, let me go, you pettifoggers! Don't you hear me say I must go to the City Hall?

FIRST LAWYER. Oh, your Honor! A moment! Let us now hear what Hugo Grotius says.

HERMAN. To the devil with both you and Hugo Grotius! What have I to do with Hugo Grotius? He was an Arminian. What in the devil have laws to do with us that people make way off in Armenia? Henrich, put them straight out the door. [Exeunt Lawyers.

SCENE 3

(Henrich remains in the entry squabbling with some one, then shoots in headfirst, followed by a man dressed up as a woman.)

WOMAN (taking the Burgomaster by the lapels of his and screaming). Oh, what kind of a government is this that passes such damnable laws that a man may have two wives? Do you think that the judgment of God isn't on you?

HERMAN. Are you mad, woman? Who the devil ever thought of such a thing?

WOMAN. Hey, hey, hey! I shall not go away until I have your heart's blood!

HERMAN. A--ah, help! Henrich! Peiter!

(Enter Peiter. He drags the woman off. Henrich, who has been hiding, finally comes on and helps him out. Exeunt struggling.)

SCENE 4

HERMAN. Henrich, there will be trouble for you if you let in any more women or lawyers after this, for both of them kill me in their own way. If any others come and want to talk to me, you must tell them to be careful not to talk Latin, as I have given it up for a special reason.

HENRICH. I have given it up, too, for just the same reason.

HERMAN. You can say that I talk only Greek.

(Another knock. Henrich goes to the door and returns with a huge bundle of papers.)

HENRICH. Here is a heap of papers from the syndics, which the burgomaster must look over and give his opinion on.

(Herman sits down at a table and fumbles among the papers.)

HERMAN. It isn't so easy to be a burgomaster as I thought, Henrich. I've got some things here to look over that the devil himself couldn't make sense of. (Begins to write, gets sweat from his brow, sits down, and scratches out what he wrote before.) Henrich!

HENRICH. Mr. Burgomaster!

HERMAN. What's that noise you are making? Can't you keep quiet?

HENRICH. I'm not moving, Mr. Burgomaster.

HERMAN (gets up, wipes his face, and throws his wig upon the floor, to see if he can think better with his head bare. He steps over the wig, kicks it to one side, sits down to write again, and calls out). Henrich!

HENRICH. Mr. Burgomaster!

HERMAN. You 'll get into trouble if you don't stand still. That's the second time you have interrupted my train of thought.

HENRICH. Honestly I didn't do anything but tuck my shirt in and measure on my leg how much too long my livery coat is.

HERMAN (gets up again and pummels his forehead with his fists to make the thoughts come). Henrich!

HENRICH. Mr. Burgomaster!

HERMAN. Go out and tell the women that are hawking oysters on the street that they mustn't yell in the street I live in, because they disturb my political deliberations.

HENRICH (calls from the doorway, three times in succession). Listen, you oyster-women! You rabble! You carrion! You shameless wenches! You married men's whores! Is there no decency in you, that you dare to yell like that in the burgomaster's street and disturb him in his business?

HERMAN. Henrich!

HENRICH. Mr. Burgomaster!

HERMAN. Shut up, you brute!

HENRICH. It does no good, anyhow, to shout any more, because the town is full of people like that, and as soon as one goes by another comes in his place and--

HERMAN. No more talk. Stand still and keep your mouth shut. (Sits down, and again scratches out what he has written; writes more, gets up, stamps in anger, and calls.) Henrich!

HENRICH. Mr. Burgomaster!

HERMAN. I wish the devil would run off with this burgomastership. Do you want to be burgomaster in my place?

HENRICH. I'd rather be damned. (Aside.) And any one who would want the office deserves to be damned.

HERMAN (tries to sit down and go on writing, but he absent-mindedly picks the wrong place and lands on the floor). Henrich!

HENRICH. Mr. Burgomaster!

HERMAN. I'm lying on the floor.

HENRICH. So I see.

HERMAN. Come help me up.

HENRICH. But the burgomaster has just said I mustn't move from where I stand.

HERMAN. That boy is damnable. (Gets up unassisted.) Isn't some one knocking?

HENRICH. Yes. (Goes to the door.) Whom do you want?

CITIZEN (off stage). I am the alderman of the hatters' guild, and I have a complaint to make to the burgomaster.

HENRICH. Here's the alderman of the hatters with some grievances.

HERMAN. Oh, I can't keep more than one thing in my head at a time.

Ask him what it is. (Henrich asks what he wants.)

CITIZEN. It's too long. I must speak to the burgomaster in person. It can be attended to in an hour, for my complaint consists of only twenty points.

HENRICH. He says he must talk to the burgomaster in person, for his point consists of only twenty complaints.

HERMAN. Oh, God help me, poor man, I am all jumbled up in my head already. Let him in.

ACT V

SCENE 5

(Enter the Citizen.)

CITIZEN. Ah, honored Burgomaster, poor man that I am, I have suffered great injustice, which the burgomaster will at once understand when he has heard about it.

HERMAN. You must put it in writing.

CITIZEN. Here it is, all written out, in four sheets.

HERMAN. Henrich! Some one is knocking again.

HENRICH. Whom do you want to talk to?

ANOTHER CITIZEN (off stage). I have a complaint to lodge before the burgomaster against the alderman of the hatters' guild.

HERMAN. Who is that, Henrich?

HENRICH. It is this man's adversary.

Herman. Make him hand you his memorial. Both you good men wait in the anteroom meanwhile.

[Exit the Citizen.

SCENE 6

HERMAN. Henrich!

HENRICH. Yes, sir!

HERMAN. Can't you help me put this to rights? I don't know what to do first. Read aloud that hatter's statement.

HENRICH (falteringly reads). "Noble, learned, stern, and steadfast Burgomaster. As the first-fruits of the worthy company of lawful citizens of this glorious city, I the undersigned, N. N., present myself, unworthy Alderman of the worthy Hatters' Guild; and after having extended congratulations both respectful and hearty on a man so worthy and highly raised on high to so height, in deepest humility submit for your consideration one of the greatest, most dangerous, and abominable abuses which wicked times and still more wicked men have brought into practice in this city, in hope that your Magnificence will afford a remedy. This, then, is the case: The hucksters here in the city, utterly without fear or shame, openly sell and offer for sale whole pieces of a sort of cloth which they cause to be woven of beaver--indeed they even descend to the dismal audacity of having stockings made of it--though it is well known that beaver-hair belongs exclusively to our profession, whereby we poor hatters are unable at any price to obtain the hair necessary for the pursuit of our means of subsistence, especially as good people have got into such a way that few will pay, as they used to do, from ten to twenty rix-dollars for a hat, to the irreparable damage of the reputation and profit of our trade. If it might now please his Magnificence the Burgomaster to consider the appended twenty-four weighty causes and reasons which have led us hat-makers presumably to presume that we alone are entitled to work in beaver, to wit:

(1) that since ancient times it has been a universal usage and custom of the country, not only this country but over the whole world, to wear beaver hats, as can be proved by manifold citations from history and by legally sworn witnesses, (a) As to history--"

HERMAN. Skip the history.

HENRICH. "(b) As to witnesses, Adrian Nilsen, in the seventy-ninth year of his age, can remember that his father's great-grandfather said--"

HERMAN. Skip what he said, too.

HENRICH. "(2) That it is an immoderate luxury to use such expensive hair for stockings and clothes, a practice at variance with all good order and usage, especially since there are so many expensive cloths imported from England, France, and Holland that one might well be satisified without depriving an honest man of his living--"

HERMAN. Enough, enough! Henrich! I see that the master is right.

HENRICH. But I have heard that an official ought always to hear both sides before he makes his decision. Shall I not read the opponents' retort also?

HERMAN. To be sure. (He hands him the other memorial.)

HENRICH (reads). "High-born Excellency, highly enlightened and highly statesmanlike Burgomaster. As high as your understanding soars above others', so high soared my joy above others' when I heard that you had become burgomaster; but what I have come for is because the hatters are annoying me and do not want to let me sell fabrics and stockings made of beaver. I understand well enough what they want: they want to have the business in beaver all to themselves and have beaver used for nothing but hats; but they do not understand the situation. It is idiotic to wear beaver hats: men go about with them under their arms, they are neither warm nor useful, and a straw hat would do just as well. On the other hand, beaver stockings and clothing are both warm and soft, and if the burgomaster had only tried them, as he may in time, he would see for himself."

HERMAN. Stop, that is enough; this man is right, too.

HENRICH. But I am sure they can't both be right.

HERMAN. Which is right, then?

HENRICH. That our Lord and the burgomaster must know.

HERMAN (gets up and walks to and fro). This is devilish nonsense, Henrich! Can't you tell me, you stupid animal, who is right? Why should I give a dog like you board and wages? (A racket outside.) What's the noise in the hall?

HENRICH. The two citizens have each other by the hair.

HERMAN. Go out and bid them respect the burgomaster's house.

HENRICH. It is better, sir, to let them fight, so they may perhaps become good friends again all the sooner. Gracious! I think they will break in; listen how they are beating on the door! (Herman crawls under the table.) Who knocks?

A LACKEY (outside). I have come from a foreign resident. My master has something to discuss with the burgomaster which is most important.

HENRICH. Where the deuce is the burgomaster? Has the devil flown off with the burgomaster? Mr. Burgomaster!

HERMAN (under the tables-whispering). Henrich! Who was that?

HENRICH. A foreign president wants to talk with your Honor.

HERMAN. Tell him to come again in half an hour, and say that there are two hat-makers here to see me whom I must despatch. Henrich! Ask the citizens to go away till to-morrow. Oh, God help me, poor man! I am so jumbled up in my head that I don't know myself what I am saying or doing. Can't you help me to get it straightened out, Henrich?

HENRICH (returning from the door), I know no better advice for his Honor than to go and hang himself.

HERMAN. Go and get me The Political Stockfish. It is lying on the sitting-room table--a German book in a white binding. Perhaps I can find in it how I should receive foreign presidents.

HENRICH. Does the burgomaster want mustard and butter with it?

HERMAN. No, it is a book in a white binding. (Exit Henrich. While he is gone Herman absent-mindedly tears the hatters' document to pieces. Reenter Henrich with the book.}

HENRICH. Here is the book. But what is it, sir, that you are tearing up? I believe it's the master hatters' complaint.

HERMAN. Oh, I did that without thinking. (He takes the book and throws it on the floor.) I believe, Henrich, I had better take your advice and hang myself.

HENRICH. Oh, Lord! Another knock! (Exit. Reenter in tears.) Oh, Mr. Burgomaster! Help, Mr. Burgomaster!

HERMAN. What's up?

HENRICH. There is a whole regiment of sailors in front of the door yelling, "If we don't get justice, we shall smash all the burgomaster's windows in." One of them hit me in the back with a stone. Oh, oh, oh!

HERMAN (crawls under the table again). Henrich, ask Madam Burgomaster to come hold them in check. They may show respect for a woman.

HENRICH. Yes, yes, you shall see how much respect sailors have for a woman. If she goes out there, they may rape her, and then you would be worse off in the end than you were in the beginning.

HERMAN. Oh, but she is an old woman.

HENRICH. Sailors aren't so particular. I shouldn't risk my wife like that. They are knocking again. Shall I open the door?

HERMAN. No, I'm afraid it's the sailors. Oh, I wish I were in my grave. Henrich, run to the door and listen to see who it is.

HENRICH. Look, they are coming right in. It is two councillors.

SCENE 7

(Enter Abrahams and Sanderus.)

ABRAHAMS. Isn't the burgomaster at home?

HENRICH. Yes, he's sitting under the table. Mr. Burgomaster!

SANDERUS. What? Are you sitting under the table, your Honor?

HERMAN. Oh, good sirs, I never asked to be made burgomaster. Why have you got me into all this trouble?

ABRAHAMS. You certainly accepted it at one time. Do come out, your Honor! We have come to point out the great wrong you did the foreign minister when you dismissed him so haughtily-because of which the city may get into difficulties. We thought that the burgomaster understood Jus publicum and ceremony better than that.

HERMAN. Oh, good gentlemen, you can depose me, and then I shall be relieved of a burden I am too weak to bear, and the foreign minister will get satisfaction at the same time.

SANDERUS. Far be it from us, your Honor, to depose you! You must come with us straight to the City Hall to consider with the syndics how the error can be remedied.

HERMAN. I won't go to the City Hall, even if I'm dragged by the hair. I don't want to be burgomaster, I never did want to be burgomaster, and I'd rather you killed me. I am a tinker, before God and honor, and a tinker I shall die.

SANDERUS. Will you make fools of the entire council? Listen, colleague, did he not accept the office of burgomaster?

ABRAHAMS. Certainly, and it is a fact which we have already reported to the council.

SANDERUS. We must consider the matter. The whole Senate is not going to allow itself to be made game of in this way. [Exeunt Abrahams and Sanderus.]

SCENE 8

HERMAN. Henrich! (He comes out from under the table.)

HENRICH. Mr. Burgomaster!

HERMAN. What do you think these councillors are going to do to me?

HENRICH. I don't know; they were very angry, I could see. I am surprised that they dared use such language in the burgomaster's own room. If I had been burgomaster, I should have come right out and said to them: "Shut up, you scurvy-necks! Stick your fingers on the floor and smell whose house you are in!"

HERMAN. I wish you were burgomaster, Henrich! I wish you were burgomaster! Oh--oh--oh'

HENRICH. If I might interrupt your business, sir, I should like to make one humble request, and that is that henceforth I might be called "von Henrich."

HERMAN. You shameless rogue! Is this the time to come to me with such talk, now, when you see that I am caught in a net of nothing but misfortunes and troublesome business!

HENRICH. On my word, I don't ask out of ambition, but only to command a little respect in the house from my fellow servants, especially from Anneke, who--

HERMAN. If you don't shut up, I'll break your neck into little pieces! Henrich!

HENRICH. Mr. Burgomaster!

HERMAN. Can't you help me get this straightened out, you stupid dog? Look here, if you don't clear up my affairs for me, there'll be trouble.

HENRICH. It's a wonder that you should ask such a thing of me, you who are such a clever man, and have been called to this high station solely on account of your wisdom.

HERMAN. Are you going to make fun of me into the bargain? (He picks up a chair and makes as if to hit him. Henrich runs out.)

SCENE 9

HERMAN (sits down with his head in his hands and ponders a long time. Then he jumps up, startled). Didn't some one knock? (Goes softly to the door, but sees no one. He sits down again, and ponders; falls to weeping, and dries his eyes with papers; he jumps up again and yells as if he were in a frenzy.) A whole pack of papers from the syndics! The alderman of the hatters! The alderman's opponent! Complaint in twenty headings! Riot of sailors! A foreign president! Impeachment by the council! Threats! Isn't there a rope here at hand? Yes, I think there really is--there's one behind the stove. (Takes the rope and prepares a noose.) It was predicted of me, that I should be elevated by my political studies. The prophecy will come true, if only the rope holds. Let the council come, then, with all their threats, I scoff at them, once I am dead. But there is one thing I could wish for--to see the author of The Political Stockfish hanged by my side with sixteen copies of The Council of State and Political Dessert hung round his neck. (Takes the book from the table and tears it apart.} You brute! You shall never mislead another honest tinker. So, that's the last bit of comfort before I die! Now I must look for a hook to hang myself from. It will be especially noteworthy to have it said after my death: "What burgomaster in Hamburg was ever more vigilant than Herman von Bremenfeld, who in his whole term of office never slept a wink?"

SCENE 10

(Herman climbs up on a chair, where he remains all through the scene. Enter Antonius.)

ANTONIUS. Here, here! What the devil are you doing?

HERMAN. I have no intention of doing anything; on the contrary, I am about to hang myself to avoid everything. If you will keep me company, it will be a pleasure to me.

ANTONIUS. Indeed I will not; but what brings you to such a desperate intention?

HERMAN. Listen, Antonius! it won't do any good to discuss it. I am to be hanged; if it doesn't happen to-day, it will happen to-morrow. I only beg, before I die, that you will pay my respects to Madam Burgomaster and the young lady, and instruct them to give me the following epitaph:
    Traveller, stand and heed!
      Here hangs
  Burgomaster von Bremenfeld,
 Who in his whole term of office
 Spent not a minute in sleep:
  Go forth and do likewise.

You may not know, dear Antonius, that I have been made burgomaster, that I have attained a position in which I don't know black from white, and where I find myself utterly incompetent; for I have observed, from the various tribulations which I have already met, that there is a great difference between being the government and criticising the government.

ANTONIUS. Ha, ha, ha, ha, ha!

HERMAN. Don't laugh at me, Antonius! It is a sin to do it.

ANTONIUS. Ha, ha, ha! Now I see how it all works out. I was at the inn just now, and I heard people there bursting with laughter over a joke which had been played on Herman von Bremen, who had been made to believe by some young men that he had been elected burgomaster, to see how he would act. That pained me through and through and I came straight here, to warn you.

HERMAN. Ah, then I'm not a burgomaster at all?

ANTONIUS. No; the story was made out of whole cloth, to show you the foolishness of arguing about high subjects that you don't understand.

HERMAN. Then it's not true about the foreign president?

ANTONIUS. Certainly not.

HERMAN. Or the master hatter either?

ANTONIUS. All fabricated.

HERMAN. Nor the sailors?

ANTONIUS. No, no.

HERMAN. To the devil with hanging, then! Geske! Engelke! Peiter! Henrich! Come here, all of you!

SCENE 11

(Enter Geske, Engelke, Peiter, Henrich.)

HERMAN. My dear wife! Go back to work; our burgomaster business is all over.

GESKE. Over?

HERMAN. If I were sure that you used that title out of malice, it would go hard with you.

HENRICH. No, indeed, I didn't, master, but it's hard to get things straight again so quickly.

HERMAN. Take hands, you two. So, that's the way. To-morrow we shall have a wedding. Henrich!

HENRICH. Mr. Burgomaster--Beg your pardon, I mean master!

HERMAN. Burn up all my political books, for I can't have them before my eyes any more, after the foolish ideas they put into my head. (To the audience.)

> To take the leading statesman's part
> Is harder far than sneering,
> For squinting at a seaman's chart
> Is not the whole of steering:
> With books on politics at hand
> A dolt may criticise,
> But judging right our fatherland

Is only for the wise.
All craftsmen who have seen my fate,
Pray, profit by its ending:
Though all's not sound within the state,
That's not our kind of mending.
And when we drop our humble tools
And set us up as thinkers,
We look the sorry lot of fools
That statesmen would as tinkers.

ERASMUS MONTANUS OR RASMUS BERG
A COMEDY IN FIVE ACTS
1731

DRAMATIS PERSONAE

JEPPE BERG, a well-to-do peasant.

NILLE, his wife.

RASMUS BERG, called ERASMUS MONTANUS, their elder son a student at the University.

JACOB, the younger son.

JERONIMUS, a wealthy freeholder.

MAGDELONE, his wife.

LISBED, their daughter, betrothed to Rasmus.

PEER, the deacon.

JESPER, the bailiff.

A Lieutenant.

NIELS, the corporal.

ACTS I, IV, AND V

SCENE: A milage street, showing Jeppe's house.

ACTS II AND III A room in Jeppe's house.

ACT I

SCENE I

(A village street showing Jeppe's house. Jeppe, with a letter in his hand.)

JEPPE. It is a shame that the deacon is not in town, for there's so much Latin in my son's letter that I can't understand. Tears come to my eyes when I think that a poor peasant's son has got so much book-learning, especially as we aren't tenants of the university. I have heard from people who know about learning that he can dispute with any clergyman alive. Oh, if only my wife and I could have the joy of hearing him preach on the hill, before we die, we shouldn't grudge all the money we have spent on him! I can see that Peer the deacon doesn't much relish the idea of my son's coming. I believe that he is afraid of Rasmus Berg. It is a terrible thing about these scholarly people. They are so jealous of each other, and no one of them can endure the thought that another is as learned as he. The good man preaches fine sermons here in the village and can talk about envy so that the tears come to my eyes; but it seems to me that he is n't entirely free from that fault himself. I can't understand why it should be so. If any one said that a neighbor of mine understood farming better than I, should I take that to heart? Should I hate my neighbor for that? No, indeed, Jeppe Berg would never do such a thing. But if here is n't Peer the deacon!

SCENE 2

(Enter Peer the Deacon.)

JEPPE. Welcome home again, Peer.

PEER. Thank you, Jeppe Berg.

JEPPE. Oh, my dear Peer, I wish you could explain to me some Latin in my son's last letter.

PEER. That's nothing! Do you think I don't understand Latin as well as your son? I am an old Academicus, I'd have you know, Jeppe Berg.

JEPPE. I know it,--I just wondered if you understood the new Latin, for that language must change, just as the language of Sjaelland has done. In my youth the people here on the hill didn't talk the way they do now; what they now call a "lackey" used to be called a "boy;" what they now call a "mysterious" used to be called a "whore;" a "mademoiselle," a "house-maid;" a "musician," a "fiddler;" and a "secretary," a "clerk." So I suppose Latin may have changed, too, since you were in Copenhagen. Will you please explain that? (Pointing to a line in the letter.} I can read the letters, but I don't get the meaning.

PEER. Your son writes that he is now studying his Logicam, Rhetoricam, and Metaphysicam.

JEPPE. What does Logicam mean?

PEER. That's his pulpit.

JEPPE. I'm glad of that. I wish he could become a pastor!

PEER. But a deacon first.

JEPPE. What is the second subject?

PEER. That is Rhetorica, which in Danish means the Ritual. The third subject must be written wrong, or else it must be in French, because if it were Latin, I could read it easily. I am able, Jeppe Berg, to recite the whole Aurora: ala, that's a wing; ancilla, a girl; barba, a beard; coena, a chamber-pot; cerevisia, ale; campana, a bell; cella, a cellar; lagena, a bottle; lana, a wolf; ancilla, a girl; janua, a door; cerevisia, butter;--

JEPPE. You must have the devil's own memory, Peer!

PEER. Yes, I never thought I should have to stay in a poverty-stricken deacon's-living so long. I could have been something else years ago, if I had been willing to tie myself to a girl. But I prefer to help myself rather than have people say of me that I got a living through my wife.

JEPPE. But, my dear Peer, here is more Latin that I can't understand. Look at this line.

PEER. Die Veneris Hafnia domum profecturus sum. That's rather high-flown, but I understand it perfectly, though any other man might cudgel his brains over it. That means in Danish: There is come profecto a lot of Russes to Copenhagen.

JEPPE. What are the Russians doing here again?

PEER. These aren't Muscovites, Jeppe Berg, but young students, who are called "Russes."

JEPPE. Oh, I see. I suppose there is a great celebration on the days when the boys get their salt and bread and become students.

PEER. When do you expect him home?

JEPPE. To-day or to-morrow. Wait a bit, my dear Peer; I will run and tell Nille to bring us out a drink of ale.

PEER. I'd rather have a glass of brandy--it's early in the day to drink ale. [Exit Jeppe into house.

SCENE 3

PEER. To tell the truth, I am not very anxious to have Rasmus Berg come home. Not that I am afraid of his learning, for I was an old student when he was still at school, getting beatings--saving your presence--on his rump. They were different fellows who graduated in my time from what they are now. I graduated from Slagelse School with Peer Monsen, Rasmus Jespersen, Christen Klim, Mads Hansen,--whom we used to call Mads Pancake in school,--Poul Iversen,--whom we called Poul Barlycorn,--all boys with bone in their skulls and beards on their chins, able to argue on any subject that might come up. I'm only a deacon, but I'm content so long as I get my daily bread and understand my office. I have made the income a deal bigger, and get more than any of my predecessors did; so my successors won't curse me in my grave. People think that there are no fine points for a deacon to know, but I can tell you a deacon's position is a hard one if you want to keep it on such a footing that it will support a man. Before my time people here in the village thought one funeral-song as good as another, but I have arranged things so that I can say to a peasant, "Which hymn will you have? This one costs so much and this one so much;" and when it comes to scattering earth on the body, "Will you have fine sand or just common or garden dirt?" Then there are various other touches that my predecessor, Deacon Christoffer, had no idea of; but he was uneducated. I can't understand how the fellow ever came to be a deacon; yet deacon he was, all the same. I tell you, Latin helps a man a great deal in every sort of business. I wouldn't give up the Latin I know for a hundred rix-dollars. It has been worth more than a hundred rix-dollars to me in my business; yes, that and a hundred more.

SCENE 4

Enter Nille and Jeppe.

NILLE (offering the deacon a glass of brandy). Your health, Peer!

PEER. Thank you, mother. I never drink brandy unless I have a stomach-ache, but I have a bad stomach most of the time.

NILLE. Do you know, Peer, my son is coming home to-day or to-morrow! You'll find him a man you can talk to, for the boy's not tongue-tied, from all I hear.

PEER. Yes, I suppose he can talk a lot of Cloister-Latin.

NILLE. Cloister-Latin? That must be the best Latin, just as cloister-linen is the best linen.

PEER. Ha, ha, ha, ha!

JEPPE. What are you laughing at, Peer?

PEER. At nothing at all, Jeppe Berg. Just another drop! Your health, mother! It's true, as you say: cloister-linen is good linen, but--

NILLE. If that linen isn't made in a cloister, why is it called cloister-linen?

PEER. Yes, that's right enough, ha, ha, ha! But won't you give me a bite to eat with my brandy?

NILLE. Here's a little bread and cheese already cut, if you will eat it. (Gets a plate from the house.)

PEER. Thank you, mother. Do you know what bread is in Latin?

NILLE. No, indeed, I don't.

PEER (eating and talking at the same time). It's called panis; genitive, pani; dative, pano; vocative, panus; ablative, pano.

JEPPE. Goodness, Peer! That language is long-winded. What is coarse bread in Latin?

PEER. That's panis gravis; and fine bread is panis finis.

JEPPE. Why, that's half Danish!

PEER. True. There are many Latin words that were originally Danish. I'll tell you why: there was once an old rector at the school in Copenhagen, called Saxo Grammatica, who improved Latin in this country, and wrote a Latin grammar, and that's why he was called Saxo Grammatica. This same Saxo greatly enriched the Latin language with Danish words, for in his day Latin was so poor that a man couldn't write one sentence which people could understand.

JEPPE. But what does that word "Grammatica" mean?

PEER. The same as "Donat." When it is bound in a Turkish cover it is called "Donat," but when it's in white parchment it's called "Grammatica," and declined just like ala.

NILLE. I never shall see how people can keep so much in their head. My head swims just from hearing them talk about it.

JEPPE. That's why learned folk usually aren't quite right in their heads.

NILLE. What nonsense! Do you think our son Rasmus Berg isn't quite right?

JEPPE. It only seems a little queer, mother, that he should write a Latin letter to me.

PEER. Jeppe's right there, certainly. That was a little foolish. It is just as if I were to talk Greek to the bailiff, to show him that I understood the language.

JEPPE. Do you know Greek, Peer?

PEER. Why, twenty years ago I could repeat the whole Litany in Greek, standing on one foot. I still remember that the last word was "Amen."

JEPPE. Oh, Peer, it will be splendid, when my son comes back, to get you two together!

PEER. If he wants to dispute with me, he will find that I can hold my own; and if he wants to have a singing match with me, he will get the worst of it. I once had a singing contest with ten deacons and beat every one of them, for I outsang them in the Credo, all ten of them. Ten years ago I was offered the position of choir-master in Our Lady's School, but I didn't want it. Why should I take it, Jeppe? Why should I leave my parish, which loves and honors me, and which I love and honor in return? I live in a place where I earn my daily bread, and where I am respected by every one. The governor himself never comes here but he sends for me at once to pass the time with him and sing for him. Last year on this occasion he gave me two marks for singing "Ut, re, mi, fa, sol." He swore that he took more pleasure in that than in the best vocal music he had heard in Copenhagen. If you give me another glass of brandy, Jeppe, I will sing the same thing for you.

JEPPE. Do, please. Pour another glass of brandy, Nille.

[Exit Nille.]

PEER. I don't sing for every one, but you are my good friend, Jeppe, whom I serve with pleasure. (He sings.) Ut, re, mi, fa, sol, la, si, ut; now down--ut, si, la, sol, fa, mi, re, ut. (Reenter Nille with brandy. He drinks.} Now you shall hear how high I can go. Ut, re, mi, fa, sol, la, si, ut, re, mi, fa, sol, la, si, ut, re--

JEPPE. Heavens! That last was fine. Our little pigs can't go any higher with a squeak.

PEER. Now I will sing rapidly: Ut, re, mi, re--No! that wasn't right. Ut, re, mi, do, re, mi, ut--No, that went wrong, too. It's cursed hard, Jeppe, to sing so fast. But there comes Monsieur Jeronimus.

SCENE 5

(Enter Jeronimus, Magdelone, and Lisbed.)

JERONIMUS. Good morning, kinsman! Have you any news from your son?

JEPPE. Yes; he is coming to-day or to-morrow.

LISBED. Oh, is it possible? Then my dream has come true.

JERONIMUS. What did you dream?

LISBED. I dreamed that I slept with him last night.

MAGEDELONE. There is something in dreams, I tell you. Dreams are not to be despised.

JERONIMUS. That's true enough, but if you girls didn't think so much about the menfolk in the daytime, you wouldn't have so many dreams about them at night. I suppose you used to dream just as much about me in the days when we were engaged, Magdelone?

MAGEDELONE. I did, indeed, but upon my word I haven't dreamed about you for some years now.

JERONIMUS. That's because your love isn't as hot now as it used to be.

LISBED. But is it possible that Rasmus Berg is coming home to-morrow?

JERONIMUS. Come, daughter, you shouldn't show that you are so much in love.

LISBED. Oh, but is it sure that he is coming home to-morrow?

JERONIMUS. Yes, yes; you hear, don't you, that's when he is coming?

LISBED. How long is it till to-morrow, father dear?

JERONIMUS. What confounded nonsense! These people in love act as if they were crazy.

LISBED. I tell you, I shall count every hour.

JERONIMUS. You should ask how long an hour is, so that people would think that you were completely mad. Stop this twaddle and let us elders talk together.--Listen, my dear Jeppe Berg! Do you think it is wise for these two young people to marry before he gets a position?

JEPPE. That is as you think best. I can support them well enough, but it would be better that he should get a position first.

JERONIMUS. I don't think it would be wise for them to marry until then. (Lisbed weeps and wails.) Fie, shame on you! It's a disgrace for a girl to carry on so!

LISBED (sobbing). Can't he get a position soon, then?

JEPPE. There's no doubt about it; he'll get a position soon enough, for from what I hear he is so learned he can read any book there is. He wrote me a Latin letter just lately.

NILLE. And, marry, it's one that can stand alone, as the deacon can tell you.

LISBED. Was it so well written?

PEER. Yes, well written for one so young. He may amount to something, Mamsell! But there's a lot left to learn. I thought I was learned, myself, at his age, but--

JEPPE. Yes, you learned folk never praise one another--

PEER. Nonsense! Do you think I am jealous of him? Before he was born I had been up for a flogging before the school three times, and when he was in the fourth form I had been eight years a deacon.

JEPPE. One man may have a better head than another; one may learn as much in a year as others in ten.

PEER. For that matter, the deacon dares set his head against any one's.

JERONIMUS. Yes, yes, you may both be right. Let us go home, children. Good-bye, Jeppe! I happened to be passing, and I thought I might as well talk to you on the way.

LISBED. Be sure to let me know as soon as he comes!

[Exeunt Jeronimus, Magdelone, and Lisbed.

SCENE 6

(Enter Jacob.)

JEPPE. What do you want, Jacob?

JACOB. Father! Have you heard the news? Rasmus Berg is back.

JEPPE. Heavens, is it possible! How does he look?

JACOB. Oh, he looks mighty learned. Rasmus Nielsen, who drove him, swears that he did nothing all the way but dispute with himself in Greek and Elamite; and sometimes with so much zeal that he struck Rasmus Nielsen in the back of the neck three or four times, with his clenched fist, shouting all the while, "Probe the Major! Probe the Major!" I suppose he must have had a dispute with a major before he started out. Part of the way he sat still and stared at the moon and the stars with such a rapt expression that he fell off the wagon three times and nearly broke his neck from sheer learning. Rasmus Nielsen laughed at that, and said to himself, "Rasmus Berg may be a wise man in the heavens, but he is a fool on earth."

JEPPE. Let us go and meet him. Come with us, dear Peer. It may be that he has forgotten his Danish and won't be able to talk anything but Latin. In that case you can be interpreter.

PEER (aside). Not if I know it! (Aloud.) I have other things to attend to.

ACT II

SCENE I

[A room in Jeppe's house. Montanus (whose stockings are falling down around his ankles).]

MONTANUS. I have been away from Copenhagen only a day, and I miss it already. If I didn't have my good books with me, I couldn't exist in the country. Studia secundas res ornant, adversis solatium praebent. I feel as if I had lost something, after going three days without a disputation. I don't know whether there are any learned folk in the village, but if there are, I shall set them to work, for I can't live without disputation. I can't talk much to my poor parents, for they are simple folk and know hardly anything beyond their catechism; so I can't find much comfort in their conversation. The deacon and the schoolmaster are said to have studied, but I don't know how much that has amounted to; still, I shall see what they are good for. My parents were astonished to see me so early, for they had not expected me to travel by night from Copenhagen. (He strikes a match, lights his pipe, and puts the bowl of his pipe through a hole he has made in his hat.) That's what they call smoking studentikos--it's a pretty good invention for any one who wants to write and smoke at the same time. (Sits down and begins to read.)

SCENE 2

(Enter Jacob. He kisses his own hand and extends it to his brother.)

JACOB. Welcome home again, my Latin brother!

MONTANUS. I am glad to see you, Jacob. But as for being your brother, that was well enough in the old days, but it will hardly do any more.

JACOB. How so? Aren't you my brother?

MONTANUS. Of course I don't deny, you rogue, that I am your brother by birth, but you must realize that you are still a peasant boy, whereas I am a Bachelor of Philosophy. But listen, Jacob,--how are my sweetheart and her father?

JACOB. Very well. They were here a while ago and asked how soon brother would be at home.

MONTANUS. Brother again! It's not from mere pride that I object, Jacob, but it simply won't do.

JACOB. Then what shall I call you, brother?

MONTANUS. You must call me "Monsieur Montanus," for that is what I am called in Copenhagen.

JACOB. If I could only keep it in my head. Was it "Monsieur Dromedarius"?

MONTANUS. Can't you hear? I say "Monsieur Montanus."

JACOB. Mossur Montanus, Mossur Montanus.

MONTANUS. That's right. "Montanus" in Latin is the same as "Berg" in Danish.

JACOB. Then can't I be called "Jacob Montanus"?

MONTANUS. When you have been to school as long as I have and passed your examinations, then you can give yourself a Latin name, too; but as long as you are a peasant boy, you must be satisfied with plain Jacob Berg. By the way, have you noticed that my sweetheart has been longing for me?

JACOB. Indeed she has. She has been very impatient at your staying away so long, brother.

MONTANUS. There you go again, yokel!

JACOB. I meant to say: Mossur's sweetheart has been impatient because brother stayed away so long.

MONTANUS. Well, I'm here now, Jacob, and all for her sake; but I shall not stay very long, for as soon as we've had the wedding I shall take her to Copenhagen with me.

JACOB. Won't Mossur take me along?

MONTANUS. What would you do there?

JACOB. I should like to look around in the world a bit.

MONTANUS. I wish you were six or seven years younger, so that I could put you into a Latin school, and then you could be a college man, too.

JABOC. No, that wouldn't do.

MONTANUS. Why not?

JABOC. If that happened, our parents would have to go begging.

MONTANUS. Hear how the fellow talks!

JACOB. Oh, I am full of ideas. If I had studied, I should have been the devil of a rogue.

MONTANUS. I have been told that you had a good head. But what else should you like to do in Copenhagen?

JACOB. I should like to see the Round Tower and the cloister where they make the linen.

MONTANUS. Ha, ha, ha! They're busy with other things besides linen-making in the cloister. But tell me, has my future father-in-law as much money as they say?

JACOB. He surely has. He is a rich old man, and owns nearly a third of the village.

MONTANUS. Have you heard whether he intends to give his daughter a dowry?

JACOB. Oh, I think he will give her a good one, especially if he once hears Mossur preach here in the village.

MONTANUS. That will never happen. I should lower myself too much by preaching here in the country. Besides, I am interested only in disputation.

JACOB. I thought it was better to be able to preach.

MONTANUS. Do you know what disputation really means?

JACOB. Of course! I dispute every day here at home with the maids, but I don't gain anything by it.

MONTANUS. Oh, we have plenty of that kind of disputation.

JACOB. What is it, then, that Mossur disputes about?

MONTANUS. I dispute about weighty and learned matters. For example: whether angels were created before men; whether the earth is round or oval; about the moon, sun, and stars, their size and distance from the earth; and other things of a like nature.

JACOB. That's not the sort of thing I dispute about, for that's not the sort of thing that concerns me. If only I can get the servants to work, they can say the world is eight-cornered, for all I care.

MONTANUS. Oh, animal brutum!--Listen, Jacob, do you suppose any one has let my sweetheart know that I have come home?

JACOB. I don't believe so.

MONTANUS. Then you had better run over to Master Jeronimus's and inform him of the event.

JACOB. Yes, I can do that, but shall I not tell Lisbed first?

MONTANUS. Lisbed? Who is that?

JACOB. Don't you know, brother, that your betrothed's name is Lisbed?

MONTANUS. Have you forgotten all I have just taught you, you rascal?

JACOB. You may call me "rascal" as much as you like, but I'm your brother just the same.

MONTANUS. If you don't shut up, I'll profecto hit you over the head with this book.

JACOB. It wouldn't be proper to throw the Bible at people.

MONTANUS. This is no Bible.

JACOB. Marry, I know a Bible when I see one. That book is big enough to be the Bible. I can see that it's not a Gospel Book, nor a Catechism. But whatever it is, it's a bad thing to throw books at your brother.

MONTANUS. Shut up, rascal!

JACOB. I may be a rascal, but I earn with my hands the money for my parents that you spend.

MONTANUS. If you don't shut up, I'll maim you. (Throws the book at him.)

JACOB. Ow, ow, ow!

SCENE 3

(Enter Jeppe and Nille.)

JEPPE. What is all this noise?

JACOB. Oh, my brother Rasmus is beating me.

NILLE. What does this mean? He wouldn't hit you without good reason.

MONTANUS. No, mother, that is so. He comes here and bandies words with me as though he were my equal.

NILLE. What a devil's own rogue! Don't you know enough to respect such a learned man? Don't you know that he is an honor to our whole family? My dear and respected son, you mustn't pay any attention to him, he is an ignorant lout.

MONTANUS. I sit here speculating about important questions, and this importunissimus and audacissimus juvenis comes and hinders me. It is no child's play to have to deal with these transcendentalibus. I wouldn't have had it happen for two marks.

JEPPE. Oh, don't be angry, my dear son! This shall never happen again. I am so much afraid that my honored son has allowed himself to get over-excited. Learned folk can't stand many shocks. I know that Peer the deacon got excited once and didn't recover for three days.

MONTANUS. Peer the deacon! Is he learned?

JEPPE. I should say he was! As far back as I can remember, we have never had a deacon here in the village who could sing as well as he can.

MONTANUS. For all that, he may have no learning at all.

JEPPE. He preaches beautifully, too.

MONTANUS. For all that, too, he might have no learning at all.

NILLE. Oh, honored son! How can a man lack learning if he preaches well?

MONTANUS. Surely, mother! All the ignorant folk preach well, for inasmuch as they can't compose anything out of their own heads, they use borrowed sermons, and learn good men's compositions by heart, though sometimes they don't understand them themselves. A learned man, on the other hand, won't use such methods; he composes out of his own head. Believe me, it is a common mistake in this country to judge a student's learning altogether too much from his sermons. But let the fellow dispute as I do--there's the touchstone of learning. If any one says this table is a candlestick, I will justify the statement. If any one says that meat or bread is straw, I will justify that, too; that has been done many a time. Listen, father! Will you admit that the man who drinks well is blessed?

JEPPE. I think rather that he is accursed, for a man can drink himself out of both reason and money.

MONTANUS. I will prove that he is blessed. Quicunque bene bibit, bene dormit. But, no,--you don't understand Latin; I must say it in Danish. Whoever drinks well, sleeps well. Isn't that so?

JEPPE. That's true enough, for when I am half-drunk I sleep like a horse.

MONTANUS. He who sleeps well does not sin. Isn't that true, too?

JEPPE. True, too; so long as a man's asleep he doesn't sin.

MONTANUS. He who does not sin is blessed.

JEPPE. That is also true.

MONTANUS. Ergo: he who drinks well is blessed.--Little mother, I will turn you into a stone.

NILLE. Oh, nonsense! That is more than even learning can do.

MONTANUS. You shall hear whether it is or not. A stone cannot fly.

NILLE. No, indeed it can't, unless it is thrown.

MONTANUS. You cannot fly.

NILLE. That is true, too.

MONTANUS. Ergo: little mother is a stone. (Nille cries.} Why are you crying, little mother?

NILLE. Oh! I am so much afraid that I shall turn into a stone. My legs already begin to feel cold.

MONTANUS. Don't worry, little mother. I will immediately turn you into a human being again. A stone neither thinks nor talks.

NILLE. That is so. I don't know whether it can think or not, but it surely cannot talk.

MONTANUS. Little mother can talk.

NILLE. Yes, thank God, I talk as well as a poor peasant woman can!

MONTANUS. Good! Ergo: little mother is no stone.

NILLE. Ah! That did me good! Now I am beginning to feel like myself again. Faith, it must take strong heads to study. I don't see how your brains can stand it.--Jacob, after this you shall wait on your brother; you have nothing else to do. If your parents see that you annoy him, you shall get as many blows as your body can stand.

MONTANUS. Little mother, I should like very much to break him of the habit of calling me "brother." It is not decent for a peasant boy to call a learned man "brother." I should like to have him call me "Monsieur."

JEPPE. Do you hear that, Jacob? When you speak to your brother after this, you are to call him Mossur.

MONTANUS. I should like to have the deacon invited here to-day, so that I can see what he is good for.

JEPPE. Yes, surely, it shall be done.

MONTANUS. In the mean time I will go to visit my sweetheart.

NILLE. But I am afraid it is going to rain. Jacob can cany your cloak for you.

MONTANUS. Jacob.

JACOB. Yes, Mossur.

MONTANUS. Walk behind me and carry my cloak.

[Exit Montanus followed by Jacob bearing the cloak.]

SCENE 4

JEPPE. Haven't we cause to be pleased with a son like that, Nille?

NILLE. Yes, indeed, not a penny has been wasted on him.

JEPPE. We shall hear to-day what the deacon is good for. But I am afraid that he won't come if he hears that Rasmus Berg is here,--there is no need of our letting him know that. We will write the bailiff, too; he is glad enough to come, for he likes our ale.

NILLE. It is very dangerous, husband, to treat the bailiff; a man like that mustn't find out how our affairs stand.

JEPPE. He is welcome to know. Every man here in the village is aware that we are well-to-do folks. As long as we pay our taxes and land rent, the bailiff can't touch a hair of our head.

NILLE. Oh, dear husband, I wonder if it is too late to let our Jacob get an education. Just think, if he could be a learned lad like his brother, what a joy it would be for his old parents!

JEPPE. No, wife, one is enough; we must have one at home who can give us a hand and do our work.

NILLE. Oh, at such work as that a man cannot do more than live from hand to mouth. Rasmus Berg, who is a scholar, can do our family more good, with his brain, in an hour than the other in a year.

JEPPE. That makes no difference, little mother; our fields must be tilled and our crops looked after. We can't possibly get along without Jacob. Look, here he is now, coming back again!

SCENE 5

Enter Jacob.

JACOB. Ha! ha, ha, ha, ha, ha, ha! My brother may be a very learned man, but he is a great simpleton for all that.

NILLE. You wicked rascal! Do you call your brother a simpleton?

JACOB. I really don't know what I ought to call such a thing, little mother. It rained until it poured, and yet he let me walk along behind him with the cloak on my arm.

JEPPE. Couldn't you have been civil enough to have said, "Mossur, it is raining. Won't you put on your cloak?"

JACOB. It seems to me, little father, it would have been very strange for me to say to the person whose parents had spent so much money upon him to teach him wisdom and cleverness, when so much rain was falling on him that he was wet to his shirt, "It is raining, sir; won't you put on your cloak?" He had no need of my warning; the rain gave him warning enough.

JEPPE. Did you walk the whole way, then, with the cloak on your arm?

JACOB. Marry, I did not; I wrapped myself up comfortably in the cloak; so my clothes are perfectly dry. I understand that sort of thing better than he, though I've not spent so much money learning wisdom. I grasped it at once, although I don't know one Latin letter from another.

JEPPE. Your brother was plunged in thought, as deeply learned folk usually are.

JACOB. Ha, ha! the devil split such learning!

JEPPE. Shut up, you rogue, or shame on your mouth! What does it matter if your brother is absent-minded about such things as that, when in so many other matters he displays his wisdom and the fruit of his studies?

JACOB. Fruit of his studies! I shall tell you what happened next on our trip. When we came to Jeronimus's gate, he went right to the side where the watch-dog stood, and he would have had his learned legs well caulked if I had not dragged him to the other side; for watch-dogs are no respecters of persons: they measure all strangers with the same stick, and bite at random whatever legs they get hold of, whether Greek or Latin. When he entered the court, Mossur Rasmus Berg absent-mindedly went into the stable and shouted, "Hey, is Jeronimus at home?" But the cows all turned their tails to him and none of them would answer a word. I am certain that if any of them could have talked, they would have said, "What a confounded lunk-head that lad must be!"

NILLE. Oh, my dear husband, can you stand hearing him use such language?

JEPPE. Jacob, you will get into trouble if you talk like that any more.

JACOB. Little father ought rather to thank me, for I set him to rights and took him out of the stable toward the house. Just think what might happen to such a lad if he should go on a long journey alone; for I'm sure that if I had not been with him, he would have been standing in the stable yet, gazing at the cows' tails, from sheer learning.

JEPPE. A plague on your impudent mouth!

[Jacob runs off, Jeppe after him.

NILLE. The confounded rogue!--I have sent word to the bailiff and the deacon, so that my son can have some one to dispute with when he comes back.

ACT III

SCENE 1

Same as Act II.

NILLE (alone). My son Montanus is gone a long time. I wish he would come home before the bailiff goes, for he wants very much to talk with him, and is eager to ask him about several things which--But there, I see him coming.

SCENE 2

Enter Montanus.

NILLE. Welcome home, my dear son. Our kind friend Jeronimus was no doubt very glad to see our honored son in good health after so long an absence.

MONTANUS. I have spoken neither to Jeronimus nor to his daughter, on account of that fellow with whom I got into a dispute.

NILLE. What kind of a man was he? Perhaps it was the schoolmaster.

MONTANUS. No, it was a stranger, who is going away to-day. I know him, although I have not associated with him in Copenhagen. I am annoyed almost to death by these people who imagine they have absorbed all wisdom, and still are idiots. I'll tell you, mother, how it is: This fellow has been ordinarius opponens once or twice; therein lies his sole achievement. But how did he perform his Partes? Misere et haesitanter absque methodo. Once when Praeses wished to distinguish inter rem et modum rei, he asked, Quid hoc est?--Wretch, you should have known that antequam in arenam descendis. Quid hoc est? Quae bruta! A fellow who ignores the distinctiones cardinales, and then wants to dispute publice!

NILLE. Oh, my respected son, you mustn't take such things as that to heart. I can see from what you say that he must be a fool.

MONTANUS. An ignoramus.

NILLE. Nothing could be plainer.

MONTANUS. An idiot.

NILLE. I can't see that he is anything else.

MONTANUS. Et quidem plane hospes in philosophia. Let the dog turn away from what he committed in the presence of so many worthy people.

NILLE. Is that what he did? By that you may know a swine.

MONTANUS. No, little mother, he did something worse than that; he openly confounded materiam cum forma.

NILLE. Plague take him!

MONTANUS. Does the fellow imagine that he can dispute?

NILLE. The devil he can!

MONTANUS. Not to mention the mistake he made in his Proemio, when he said "Lectissimi et doctissimi auditores."

NILLE. What a fool he must be!

MONTANUS. For putting "lectissimi" in front of "doctissimi," when "lectissimi" is a predicate, one can give a Deposituro.

NILLE. But didn't you get a chance to talk with Jeronimus, my son?

MONTANUS. No, just as I was about to go into the house, I saw the fellow passing by the gate, and as we knew each other, I went out to speak to him, whereupon we immediately began to talk of learned matters, and finally to dispute, so that I had to postpone my visit.

NILLE. I am very much afraid that Monsieur Jeronimus will be offended when he hears that my son has been in his yard, but went away without talking with him.

MONTANUS. Well, I can't help that. When any one attacks philosophy, he attacks my honor. I am fond of Mademoiselle Lisbed, but my Metaphysica and my Logica have priority.

NILLE. Oh, my dear son, what did I hear? Are you engaged to two other girls in Copenhagen? That will be a bad business in the matrimonial courts.

MONTANURS. You don't understand me; I didn't mean it in that way. They are not two girls, but two sciences.

NILLE. Oh, that is another matter. But here comes the bailiff. Don't be angry any more.

MONTANUS. I can't be angry with him, for he is a simple, ignorant man, with whom I cannot get into a dispute.

SCENE 3

Enter Jeppe and Jesper the Bailiff.

JEPPE. Serviteur, Monsieur. I congratulate you on your arrival.

MONTANUS. I thank you, Mr. Bailiff.

JESPER. I am glad that we have such a learned man here in the village. It must have cost you many a racking of the brain to have advanced so far. I congratulate you, too, Jeppe Berg, upon your son. Now, happiness has come to you in your old age.

JEPPE. Yes, that is true.

JESPER. But listen, my dear Monsieur Rasmus, I should like to ask you something.

MONTANUS. My name is Montanus.

JESPER (aside to Jeppe). Montanus? is that the Latin for Rasmus?

JEPPE. Yes, it must be.

JESPER. Listen, my dear Monsieur Montanus Berg. I have heard that learned folk have such extraordinary ideas. Is it true that people in Copenhagen think the earth is round? Here on the hill no one believes it; for how can that be, when the earth looks perfectly flat?

MONTANUS. That is because the earth is so large that one cannot notice its roundness.

JESPER. Yes, it is true, the earth is large; it is almost a half of the universe. But listen, Monsieur, how many stars will it take to make a moon?

MONTANUS. A moon! In comparison to the stars the moon is like Pebling Pond in comparison with all Sjaelland.

JESPER. Ha, ha, ha! Learned folk are never just right in the head. Will you believe it, I have heard people say that the earth moves and the sun stands still. You certainly don't believe that, too, Monsieur?

MONTANUS. No man of sense doubts it any longer.

JESPER. Ha, ha, ha! If the earth should move, surely we should fall and break our necks.

MONTANUS. Can't a ship move with you, without your breaking your neck?

JESPER. Yes, but you say that the earth turns round. Now. if a ship should turn over, wouldn't the people fall off then into the sea?

MONTANUS. No. I will explain it to you more plainly, if you will have the patience.

JESPER. Indeed, I won't hear anything about it. I should have to be crazy to believe such a thing. Could the earth turn over, and we not fall heels over head to the devil and clear down into the abyss? Ha, ha, ha! But, my Monsieur Berg, how is it that the moon is sometimes so small and sometimes so big?

MONTANUS. If I tell you why, you won't believe me.

JESPER. Oh, please tell me.

MONTANUS. It is because, when the moon has grown large, pieces are clipped off it to make stars of.

JESPER. That certainly is curious. I really didn't know that before. If pieces were not clipped off, it would get too large and grow as broad as all Sjaelland. After all, nature does regulate everything very wisely. But how is it that the moon doesn't give warmth like the sun, although it is just as big?

MONTANUS. That is because the moon is not a light, but made of the same dark material as the earth, and gets its light and brilliance from the sun.

JESPER. Ha, ha, ha, ha, ha, ha! Let us talk of something else. That's stuff and nonsense; a man might go stark mad over it.

SCENE 4

(Enter Peer.)

JEPPE. Welcome, Peer. Where good folk are gathered, good folk come. Here, you see, is my son, who has just come back.

PEER. Welcome, Monsieur Rasmus Berg!

MONTANUS. In Copenhagen, I am accustomed to be called "Montanus." I beg you to call me that.

PEER. Yes, surely, it's all the same to me. How are things in Copenhagen? Did many graduate this year?

MONTANUS. About as many as usual.

PEER. Was any one rejected this year?

MONTANUS. Two or three conditionaliter.

PEER. Who is Imprimatur this year?

MONTANUS. What does that mean?

PEER. I mean, who is Imprimatur of the verse and the books which are published?

MONTANUS. Is that supposed to be Latin?

PEER. Yes, in my day it was good Latin.

MONTANUS. If it was good Latin then, it must be so still. But it has never been Latin in the sense in which you use it.

PEER. Yes, it is,--good Latin.

MONTANUS. Is it a nomen or a verbum?

PEER. It is a nomen.

JESPER. That is right, Peer, just speak up for yourself.

MONTANUS. Cuius declinationis is Imprimatur, then?

PEER. All the words that can be mentioned may be referred to eight things, which are: nomen, pronomen, verbum, principium, conjugatio, declinatio, interjectio.

JESPER. Yes, yes, just listen to Peer when he shakes his sleeves! That's right, keep at him!

MONTANUS. He's not answering what I ask him. What is the genitive of "Imprimatur"?

PEER. Nominativus, ala; genitivus, alae; dativus, ala; vocativus, ala; ablativus, ala.

JESPER. Ah, ha, Monsieur Montanus, we have some folk here on the hill, too!

PEER. I should say so. In my time the fellows that graduated were of a different sort from nowadays. They were lads who got shaved twice a week, and could scan all kinds of verse.

MONTANUS. That is certainly a wonderful thing! Boys in the second class can do that to-day. Nowadays there are graduates from the schools in Copenhagen who can write Hebrew and Chaldean verse,

PEER. Then they can't know much Latin.

MONTANUS. Latin! If you went to school now, you couldn't get above the bottom class.

JESPER. Don't say that, Montanus. The deacon is, I know, a thoroughly educated man; that I have heard both the district bailiff and the tax-collector say.

MONTANUS. Perhaps they understand Latin just as little as he

JESPER. But I can hear that he answers splendidly.

MONTANUS. Yes, but he doesn't answer what I ask him--E qua schola dimissus es, mi Domine?

PEER. Adjectivum et substantivum genere, numero et caseo conveniunt.

JESPER. He's giving him his bucket full. Good for you, Peer; as sure as you live, we shall drink a half pint of handy together.

MONTANUS. If you knew, Mr. Bailiff, what his answers were, you would laugh until you split. I ask him from what school he graduated and he answers at random something entirely different.

PEER. Tunc tua res agitur, paries cum proximus ardet.

JESPER. Yes, yes, that's a good lead for you. Answer that, now.

MONTANUS. I can't answer that; it is mere mincemeat. Let us talk Danish, so the others can understand; then you will be able to hear what kind of a fellow he is. (Nille cries.)

JESPER. What are you crying for, my good woman?

NILLE. Oh, I am so sorry that my son must admit himself beaten in Latin.

JESPER. Oh, it's no wonder, my good woman. Peer is, of course, much older than he; it is no wonder. Let them talk Danish, then, as we all understand it.

PEER. Yes, certainly. I am ready for whichever one of the two he wishes. We shall propose certain questions to each other; for example, who was it that screamed so loud that he could be heard over the whole world?

MONTANUS. I know no one who screams louder than asses and country deacons.

PEER. Nonsense! Can they be heard over the whole world? It was the ass in Noah's ark; for the whole world was in the ark.

JESPER. Ha, ha, ha! That is true, to be sure. Ha, ha, ha! Peer the deacon has a fine head on his shoulders.

PEER. Who was it killed a quarter of the world?

MONTANUS. Bah! I refuse to answer such stupid questions.

PEER. It was Cain, who killed his brother Abel.

MONTANUS. Prove that there were no more than four human beings at the time. of course, much older than he; it is no wonder. Let them talk Danish, then, as we all understand it.

PEER. You prove that there were more.

MONTANUS. That isn't necessary; for affirmante incumbit probatio. Do you understand that?

PEER. Of course I do. Omnia conando docilis solertia vincit. Do you understand that?

MONTANUS. I am a perfect fool to stand here and dispute with a dunce. You wish to dispute, and yet know neither Latin nor Danish; much less do you know what logic is. Let's hear once, quid est logica?

PEER. Post molestam senectutam, post molestam senectutam nos habebat humus.

MONTANUS. Are you trying to make a fool of me, you rascal? (He grabs him by the hair. The Deacon escapes and shouts, "Dunce, dunce!") [Exeunt all except the Bailiff.]

SCENE 5

(Enter Jeronimus.)

JERONIMUS. Your servant, Mr. Bailiff. I am surprised to find you here. I have come to see my future son-in-law, Rasmus Berg.

JESPER. He will be here in a moment. It is a shame that you didn't come a half hour sooner. You would then have heard him and the deacon disputing together.

JERONIMUS. How did it come out?

JESPER. Shame on Peer the deacon! He is worse than I thought. I see well enough that he has forgot nothing either of his Latin or Hebrew.

JERONIMUS. I believe that well enough, for he probably never knew much of either.

JESPER. Don't say that, Monsieur Jeronimus! He has a devilish clever tongue. It is really a joy to hear the man talk Latin.

JERONIMUS. That is more than I should have expected. But how does my son look?

JESPER. He looks confoundedly learned. You would hardly recognize him. He has another name, too.

JERONIMUS. Another name! What does he call himself?

JESPER. He calls himself Montanus, which is said to be the same as Rasmus in Latin.

JERONIMUS. Oh, shame! that is wicked. I have known many who have changed their Christian names in that way, but they never have prospered. Some years ago I knew a person who was christened Peer, and afterwards, when he had become a man of consequence, wanted to be coined again, and called himself Peter. But that name cost him dear, for he broke his leg and died in great misery. Our Lord doesn't allow such a thing, Mr. Bailiff.

JESPER. I don't care what his name is, but I don't like it that he has such peculiar opinions in religion.

JERONIMUS. What kind of opinions has he, then?

JESPER. Oh, it's terrible! My hair stands on end when I think of it. I can't remember all that I heard, but I know that among other things he said that the earth was round. What can I call such a thing, Monsieur Jeronimus? That is nothing else than overthrowing all religion and leading folk away from the faith. A heathen certainly cannot speak worse.

JERONIMUS. He must have said that only in jest.

JESPER. It is going rather too far to joke about such things as that. See, here he comes himself.

SCENE 6

(Enter Montanus.)

MONTANUS. How do you do, my dear father-in-law. I am delighted to see you in good health.

JERONIMUS. People of my age can't enjoy remarkable health.

MONTANUS. You look mighty well, however.

JERONIMUS. Do you think so?

MONTANUS. How is Miss Lisbed?

JERONIMUS. Oh, well enough.

MONTANUS. But what is the matter? It seems to me, my dear father-in-law, that you answer me rather coldly.

JERONIMUS. I have no good reason to do otherwise.

MONTANUS. What wrong have I done?

JERONIMUS. I have been told that you have such peculiar opinions that people might really think that you had become mad or deranged, for how can a sane man be foolish enough to say that the earth is round?

MONTANUS. But, profecto, it is round. I must speak the truth.

JERONIMUS. The deuce it is the truth! Such a notion can't possibly come from anywhere but from the devil, who is the father of lies. I am sure there isn't a single man here in the village who would not condemn such an opinion. Just ask the bailiff, who is an intelligent man, if he does not agree with me.

JESPER. It is really all one to me whether it is oblong or round; but I must believe my own eyes, which show me that the earth is as flat as a pancake.

MONTANUS. It is all one to me, too, what the bailiff or the others here in the village think on the subject; for I know that the earth is round.

JERONIMUS. The deuce it is round! You must be crazy. You surely have eyes in your head as well as other men.

MONTANUS. It is known for certain, my dear father-in-law, that people live right under us with their feet turned toward ours.

JESPER. Ha, ha, ha; hi, hi, hi; ha, ha, ha!

JERONIMUS. Yes, you may well laugh, Mr. Bailiff, for he really has a screw loose in his head. Just you try to walk here on the ceiling with your head down, and see then what will happen.

MONTANUS. That is an entirely different thing, father-in-law, because--

JERONIMUS. I will never in the world be your father-in-law. I love my daughter too well to throw her away like that.

MONTANUS. I love your daughter as my own soul, but that I should give up my philosophy for her sake and drive my reason into exile,--that is more than you can demand.

JERONIMUS. Ha, ha! I see you have another lady-love in mind. You can keep your Lucy or your Sophy. I certainly shall not force my daughter on you.

MONTANUS. You mistake me. Philosophy is nothing other than a science, which has opened my eyes, in this respect as in others.

JERONIMUS. It has rather blinded both your eyes and your understanding. How can you believe such a thing is good?

MONTANUS. That is something which is beyond proof. No learned man doubts that any longer.

JESPER. I warrant you will never get Peer the deacon to agree with you.

MONTANUS. Peer the deacon! Yes, he is a great fellow. I am a fool to stand here and talk about philosophy with you. But in order to please Monsieur Jeronimus, I will nevertheless present one or two proofs. First, we learn it from travellers, who, when they go a few thousand miles from here, have day while we have night: they see other heavens, other stars.

JERONIMUS. Are you crazy? Is there more than one heaven and one earth?

JESPER. Yes, indeed, Monsieur Jeronimus, there are twelve heavens, one above the other, until the crystal heaven is reached. So far he is right.

MONTANUS. Ah! Quantae tenebrae!

JERONIMUS. In my youth I went sixteen times to the neighborhood of Kiel, but as sure as I am an honorable man, I never saw a different heaven from what we have here.

MONTANUS. You must travel sixteen times as far, Domine Jeronime, before you can notice such a thing, because--

JERONIMUS. Stop talking such nonsense; it is neither here nor there. Let's hear your other proof.

MONTANUS. The other proof is taken from the eclipse of the sun and moon.

JESPER. Just hear that! Now, he is stark mad.

MONTANUS. What do you really suppose an eclipse to be?

JESPER. Eclipses are certain signs which are placed upon the sun and moon when some misfortune is going to happen on the earth,--a thing I can prove from my own experience: when my wife had a miscarriage three years ago, and when my daughter Gertrude died, both times there were eclipses just before.

MONTANUS. Oh, such nonsense will drive me mad.

JERONIMUS, The bailiff is right, for an eclipse never occurs unless it is a warning of something. When the last eclipse happened, everything seemed to be well, but that didn't last long; for a fortnight afterwards we got news from Copenhagen that six candidates for degrees were rejected at one time, all persons belonging to the gentry, and two of them the sons of deacons. If a man doesn't hear of misfortune at one place after such an eclipse, he hears of it at another.

MONTANUS. That is true enough, for no day passes that some misfortune does not happen somewhere in the world. But as far as these persons you mentioned are concerned, they have no need to blame the eclipse, for if they had studied more, they would have passed.

JERONIMUS. What is an eclipse of the moon, then?

MONTANUS. It is nothing other than the earth's shadow, which deprives the moon of the sunlight, and since the shadow is round, we thereby see that the earth is round, too. It all happens in a natural way, for eclipses can be predicted, and therefore it is folly to say that such are prophetic warnings of misfortune.

JERONIMUS. Oh, Mr. Bailiff, I feel ill. Unlucky was the far on which your parents allowed you to become a scholar.

JESPER. Yes, he comes mighty near to being an atheist. I must bring him and Peer the deacon together again. There is a man who speaks with force. He will persuade you yet, in either Latin or Greek, that the earth, thank God, is as flat as my hand. But here comes Madame Jeronimus with her daughter.

SCENE 7

(Enter Magdelone and Lisbed.)

MAGDELONE. Oh, my dear son-in-law, it is a delight to me to see you back again in good health.

LISBED. Oh, my darling, let me hug you.

JERONIMUS. Slowly, slowly, my child, not so ardently.

LISBED. May I not hug my sweetheart when I haven't seen him for years?

JERONIMUS. Keep away from him, I tell you, or else you will get a beating.

LISBED (weeping). I know one thing, that we have been publicly betrothed.

JERONIMUS. That is true enough, but since that time something has occurred to hinder. (Lisbed weeps.) You must know, my child, that when he became engaged to you he was an honest man and a good Christian. But now he is a heretic and a fanatic, who ought to be introduced to the Litany rather than into our family.

LISBED. If that is all, father dear, we can still make everything right.

JERONIMUS. Keep away from him, I tell you.

MAGDELONE. What does this mean, Mr. Bailiff?

JESPER. It's a bad business, Madame. He introduces false doctrine into this village, saying that the earth is round, and other things of such a nature that I should blush to mention them.

JERONIMUS. Don't you think that the good old parents are to be pitied who have spent so much money on him?

MAGDELONE. Oh, is that all? If he loves our daughter, he will give up his opinion and say that the earth is flat, for her sake.

LISBED. Oh, my dear, for my sake say that it is flat!

MONTANUS. I cannot humor you in this, so long as I am in full possession of my reason. I cannot give the earth another shape from what it has by nature. For your sake I will say and do whatever is possible for me; but in this one thing I can never humor you, for if the brothers in my order should find out that I had given expression to such an opinion, I should be thought a fool, and despised. Besides, we learned folk never give up our opinions, but defend what we have once said to the uttermost drop of our inkhorns.

MAGDELONE. See here, husband, I don't think it matters so much that we should break off the match on that account.

JERONIMUS. And merely on that account I should try to have them divorced even if they had been actually married.

MAGEDELONE. You had better believe I have something to say in this matter, too; for if she is your daughter, she is mine as well.

LISBED (weeping). Oh, my dear, do say that it is flat.

MONTANUS. Profecto, I really cannot.

JERONIMUS. Listen, wife: you must know that I am the head of the house, and that I am her father.

MAGDELONE. You must also know that I am the mistress of the house, and that I am her mother.

JERONIMUS. I say that a father is always more than a mother.

MAGDELONE, And I say not, for there can be no doubt that I am her mother, but whether you--I had better not say any more, for I am getting excited.

LISBED (weeping). Oh, my heart, can't you say just for my sake that it is flat?

MONTANUS. I cannot, my doll, nam contra naturam est.

JERONIMUS. What did you mean by that, my wife? Am I not her father as surely as you are her mother?--Listen, Lisbed, am I not your father?

LISBED. I think so, for my mother says so; but I know that she is my mother.

JERONIMUS. What do you think of this talk, Mr. Bailiff:

JESPER. I can't say that Mamselle is wrong in this matter, for--

JERONIMUS. That is enough. Come, let us go--you may be sure, my good Rasmus Berg, that you will never get my daughter so long as you cling to your delusions.

LISBED (weeping). Oh, my heart, do say that it is flat!

JERONIMUS. Out, out of the door!

[Exeunt Jeronimus, Magdelone, and Lisbed.]

ACT IV

SCENE I

(Before Jeppe's House.)

MONTANUS. Here I have been worried for a good hour by my parents, who with sighing and weeping try to persuade me to give up my opinions; but they don't know Erasmus Montanus. Not if I were to be made an emperor for it would I renounce what I once have said. I love Mademoiselle Elisabet, to be sure; but that I should sacrifice philosophy for her sake, and repudiate what I have publicly maintained--that is out of the question. I hope, though, that it will all come out right, and that I shall win my sweetheart without losing my reputation. Once I get a chance to talk to Jeronimus, I can convince him of his errors so conclusively that he will agree to the match. But there are the deacon and the bailiff, coming from my father- and mother-in-law's.

SCENE 2

(Enter Peer and Jesper.)

JESPER. My dear Monsieur Montanus, we have been working hard for you this day.

MONTANUS. What's that?

JESPER. We have intervened between your parents and your parents-in-law to bring about a reconciliation.

MONTANUS. Well, what have you accomplished? Did my father-in-law give way?

JESPER. The last words he said to us were, "There has never been any heresy in our family. You tell Rasmus Berg"--I merely quote his words; he never once said Montanus Berg--"You tell Rasmus Berg from me," said he, "that my wife and I are both honest, God-fearing people, who would rather wring our daughter's neck than marry her to any one who says that the earth is round, and brings false doctrine into the village."

PEER. To tell the truth, we have always had pure faith here on the hill, and Monsieur Jeronimus isn't far wrong in wishing to break off the match.

MONTANUS. My good friends, tell Monsieur Jeronimus from me that he is committing a sin in attempting to force me to repudiate what I once have said--a thing contrary to leges scholasticas and consuetudines laudabiles.

PEER. Oh, Dominus! Will you give up your pretty sweetheart for such trifles? Every one will speak ill of it.

MONTANUS, The common man, vulgus, will speak ill of it; but my commilitiones, my comrades, will praise me to the skies for my constancy.

PEER. Do you consider it a sin to say that the earth is flat or oblong?

MONTANUS. No, I do not, but I consider it shameful and dishonorable for me, a Baccalaureus Philosophiae, to repudiate what I have publicly maintained, and to do anything that is improper for one of my order. My duty is to see to it that ne quid detrimenti patiatur respublica philosophica.

PEER. But if you can be convinced that what you believe is false, do you consider it a sin to give up your opinion?

MONTANUS. Prove to me that it is false, and that methodice.

PEER. That is an easy thing for me to do. Now, a great many fine people live here in the village: first, your father-in-law, who has become distinguished by the mere use of his pen; next, myself, unworthy man, who have been deacon here for fourteen full years; then this good man, the bailiff, besides the parish constable, and various other good men established here who have paid their taxes and land rent in both good times and bad.

MONTANUS. That's the deuce of a syllogismus. What does all such nonsense lead to?

PEER. I'm coming to that directly. I say, just ask any one of these good men who live here in the village and see if any of them will agree with you that the world is round. I'm sure a man ought to believe what so many say, rather than what only one says. Ergo, you are wrong.

MONTANUS. You may bring all the people on the hill and let them oppose me both in this matter and others, and I shall close the mouths of all of them. Such people have no convictions; they must believe what I and other folk say.

PEER. But if you should say the moon was made of green cheese, would they believe that, too?

MONTANUS. Why not? Tell me, what do the people here think you are?

PEER. They believe that I am a good, honest man and deacon here in this place; which is true.

MONTANUS. And I say it is a lie. I say you are a cock, and I shall prove it, as surely as two and three make five.

PEER. The devil you will! Now, how can I be a cock? How can you prove that?

MONTANUS. Can you tell me anything to prevent you from being one?

PEER. In the first place I can talk; a cock cannot talk; ergo, I am not a cock.

MONTANUS. Talking does not prove anything. A parrot or a starling can talk, too; that does not make them human beings by any means.

PEER. I can prove it from something else besides talking. A cock has no human intelligence. I have human intelligence; ergo, I am not a cock.

MONTANUS. Proba minorem.

JESPER. Aw, talk Danish.

MONTANUS. I want him to prove that he has the intelligence of a human being.

PEER. See here, I discharge the duties of my office irreproachably, don't I?

MONTANUS. What are the main duties of your office wherein you show human intelligence?

PEER. First, I never forget to ring for service at the hour appointed.

MONTANUS. Nor does a cock forget to crow and make known the hour and tell people when to get up.

PEER. Second, I can sing as well as any deacon in Sjaelland.

MONTANUS. And our cock crows as well as any cock in Sjaelland.

PEER. I can mould wax candles, which no cock can do.

MONTANUS. Over against that, a cock can make a hen lay eggs, which you can't do. Don't you see that the intelligence you show in your calling fails to prove that you are better than a cock? Let us see, in a nutshell, what points you have in common with a cock: a cock has a comb on his head, you have horns on your forehead; a cockcrows, you crow, too; a cock is proud of his voice and ruffles himself up, you do likewise; a cock gives warning when it is time to get up, you when it is time for service. Ergo, you are a cock. Have you anything else to say? (Peer cries.)

JESPER. Here, don't cry, Peer! Why do you heed such things?

PEER. A plague on me if it's not sheer falsehood. I can get a certificate from the whole village that I am not a rooster; that not one of my forbears has been anything but a Christian human being.

MONTANUS, Refute, then, this syllogismus, quem tibi propano. A cock has certain peculiarities which distinguish him from other animals: he wakes people by a noise when it's time to get up; announces the hours; plumes himself on his voice; wears protuberances on his head. You have the same peculiarities. Ergo, you are a cock. Refute me that argument. (Peer weeps again.)

JESPER. If the deacon can't shut you up, I can.

MONTANUS. Let us hear your argument, then!

JESPER. First, my conscience tells me that your opinion is false.

MONTANUS. One cannot pass judgment in all matters according to a bailiff's conscience.

JESPER. In the second place, I say that everything you have said is sheer falsehood.

MONTANUS. Prove it.

JESPER. In the third place, I am an honest man, whose word has always deserved to be believed.

MONTANUS. That sort of talk will convince no one.

JESPER. In the fourth place, I say that you have spoken like a knave and that the tongue ought to be cut out of your mouth.

MONTANUS. I still hear no proof.

JESPER. And, finally, in the fifth place, I will prove it to you abundantly either with swords or with bare fists.

MONTANUS. No, I do not care for either, thank you; but as long as you wish to dispute with the mouth only, you shall find that I can justify not only the things which I have said, but more, too. Come on, Mr, Bailiff, I will prove by sound logic that you are a bull.

JESPER. The devil you will.

MONTANUS. Just have the patience to hear my argument.

JESPER. Come, Peer, let's go.

MONTANUS. I prove it in this way. Quicunque--(Jesper shrieks and puts his band over Erasmus's mouth.) If you do not wish to hear my proof this time, you can meet me another time, whenever you please.

JESPER. I am too good to associate with such a fanatic.

[Exeunt Jesper and Peer.]

SCENE 3

MONTANUS. I can dispute dispassionately with these people, however harshly they speak to me. I do not become hot-headed unless I dispute with people who imagine that they understand Methodum disputandi and that they are just as well versed in philosophy as I. For this reason I was ten times as zealous when I argued against the student to-day; for he had some appearance of learning. But here come my parents.

SCENE 4

(Enter Jeppe and Nille.)

JEPPE. Oh, my dear son, don't carry on so, and don't quarrel with everybody. The bailiff and deacon, who at our request undertook to make peace between you and your father-in-law, have, I hear, been made sport of. What is the use of turning good folk into cocks and bulls?

MONTANUS. For this purpose I have studied, for this purpose I have racked my brains: that I may say what I choose, and justify it.

JEPPE. It seems to me that it would have been better never to have studied in that way.

MONTANUS. Keep your mouth shut, old man!

JEPPE. You're not going to beat your parents?

MONTANUS. If I did, I should justify that, too, before the whole world. [Exeunt Jeppe and Nille, weeping.]

SCENE 5

(Enter Jacob.)

MONTANUS. I will not abandon my opinions, even if they all go mad at once.

JACOB. I have a letter for Mossur.

[Gives him the letter, and exit.]

SCENE 6

MONTANUS (reading). My dearest friend! I could never have imagined that you would so easily abandon her who for so many years has loved you with such faith and constancy. I can tell you for a certainty that my father is so set against the notion that the earth is round, and considers it such an important article of faith, that he will never give me to you unless you assent to the belief that be and the other good folk here in the village hold. What difference can it make to you whether the earth is oblong, round, eight-cornered, or square? I beg of you, by all the love I have borne you, that you conform to the faith in which we here on the hill have been happy for so long. If you do not humor me in this, you may be sure that I shall die of grief, and the whole world will abhor you for causing the death of one who has loved you as her own soul.

> Elisabeth, daughter of Jeronimus,
> by her own hand.

Oh, heavens! This letter moves me and throws me into great irresolution--

> Utque securi
> Saucia trabs ingens, ubi plaga novissima restat,
> Quo cadat in dubio est, omnique a parte timetur,
> Sic animus--

On the one hand is Philosophy, bidding me stand firm; on the other, my sweetheart reproaching me with coldness and faithlessness. But should Erasmus Montanus for any reason renounce his conviction, hitherto his one virtue? No, indeed, by no means. Yet here is necessity, which knows no law. If I do not submit in this, I shall make both myself and my sweetheart miserable. She will die of grief, and all the world will hate me and reproach me with my faithlessness. Ought I abandon her, when she has loved me constantly for so many years? Ought I be the cause of her death? No, that must not be. Still, consider what you are doing, Erasmus Montane, Musarum et Apollonis pulle! Here you have the chance to show that you are a true philosophus. The greater the danger, the larger the laurel wreath you win inter philosophos. Think what your commilitiones will say when they hear something like this: "He is no longer the Erasmus Montanus who hitherto has defended his opinions to the last drop of his blood." If common and ignorant people reproach me with unfaithfulness to my sweetheart, philosophi, for their part, will exalt me to the skies. The very thing which disgraces me in the eyes of the one party crowns me with honor among the other. I must therefore resist the temptation. I am resisting it. I conquer it. I have already conquered it. The earth is round. Jacta est alea. Dixi. (Calls.) Jacob!

SCENE 7

(Enter Jacob.)

MONTANUS. Jacob, the letter which you delivered to me from my sweetheart has had no influence upon me. I adhere to what I have said. The earth is round, and it shall never become flat as long as my head remains on my shoulders.

JACOB. I believe, too, that the earth is round, but if any one gave me a seed-cake to say it was oblong, I should say that it was oblong, for it would make no difference to me.

MONTANUS. That might be proper for you, but not for a philosophus whose principal virtue is to justify to the uttermost what he once has said. I will dispute publicly on the subject here in the village and challenge all who have studied.

JACOB. But might I ask Mossur one thing: If you win the disputation, what will be the result?

MONTANUS. The result will be that I shall have the honor of winning and shall be recognized as a learned man.

JACOB. Mossur means a talkative man. I have noticed, from people here in the village, that wisdom and talking are not the same thing. Rasmus Hansen, who is always talking, and whom no one can stand against in the matter of words, is granted by every one to have just plain goose sense. On the other hand, the parish constable, Niels Christensen, who says little and always gives in, is admitted to have an understanding of the duties of chief bailiff.

MONTANUS. Will you listen to the rascal? Faith, he's trying to argue with me.

JACOB. Mossur mustn't take offence. I talk only according to my simple understanding, and ask only in order to learn. I should like to know whether, when Mossur wins the dispute, Peer the deacon will thereupon be turned a cock?

MONTANUS. Nonsense! He will stay the same as he before.

JACOB. Well, then Mossur would lose!

MONTANUS. I shall not allow myself to be drawn into dispute with a rogue of a peasant like you. If you understood Latin, I should readily oblige you. I am not accustomed to disputation in Danish.

JACOB. That is to say, Mossur has become so learned that he cannot make clear his meaning in his mother-tongue.

MONTANUS. Be silent, audacissime juvenis! Why should I exert myself to explain my opinions to coarse and common folk, who don't know what universalia entia rationis formae substantiales are? It certainly is absurdissimum to try to prate of colors to the blind. Vulgus indoctum est monstrum horrendum informe, cui lumen ademptum. Not long ago a man ten times as learned as you wished to dispute with me, but when I found that he did not know what quidditas was, I promptly refused him.

JACOB. What does that word quidditas mean? Wasn't that it?

MONTANUS. I know well enough what it means.

JACOB. Perhaps Mossur knows it himself, but can't explain it to others. What little I know, I know in such a way that all men can grasp it when I say it to them.

MONTANUS. Yes, you are a learned fellow, Jacob. What do you know?

JACOB. What if I could prove that I am more learned than Mossur?

MONTANUS. I should like to hear you.

JACOB. He who studies the most important things, I think, has the most thorough learning.

MONTANUS. Yes, that is true enough.

JACOB. I study farming and the cultivation of the soil. For that reason I am more learned than Mossur.

MONTANUS. Do you believe that rough peasants' work is the most important?

JACOB. I don't know about that. But I do know that if we farmers should take a pen or a piece of chalk in our hands to calculate how far it is to the moon, you learned men would soon suffer in the stomach. You scholars spend the time disputing whether the earth is round, square, or eight-cornered, and we study how to keep the earth in repair. Does Mossur see now that our studies are more useful and important than his, and, therefore, Niels Christensen is the most learned man here in the village, because he has improved his farm so that an acre of it is rated at thirty rix-dollars more than in the time of his predecessor, who sat all day with a pipe in his mouth, smudging and rumpling Doctor Arent Hvitfeld's Chronicle or a book of sermons?

MONTANUS. You will be the death of me; it is the devil incarnate who is talking. I never in all my life thought such words could come from a peasant-boy's mouth. For although all you have said is false and ungodly, still it is an unusual speech for one in your walk of life. Tell me this minute from whom you have learned such nonsense.

JACOB. I have not studied, Mossur, but people say I have a good head. The district judge never comes town but he sends for me at once. He has told my parents a hundred times that I ought to devote myself to books, and that something great might be made of me. When I have nothing to do, I go speculating. The other day I made a verse on Morten Nielsen, who drank himself to death.

MONTANUS. Let us hear the verse.

JACOB. You must know, first, that the father and the grandfather of this same Morten were both fishermen, and were drowned at sea. This was how the verse went:

> Here lies the body of Morten Nielsen;
> To follow the footsteps of his forbears,
> Who died in the water as fishermen,
> He drowned himself in brandy.

I had to read the verse before the district judge the other day, and he had it written down and gave me two marks for it.

MONTANUS. The poem, though formaliter very bad, is none the less materialiter excellent. The prosody, which is the most important thing, is lacking.

JACOB. What does that mean?

MONTANUS. Certain lines have not pedes, or feet, enough to walk on.

JACOB. Feet! I would have you know that in a few days it ran over the whole countryside.

MONTANUS. I see you have a crafty head. I could wish that you had studied and understood your Philosophiam instrumentalem, so you could dispute under me. Come, let us go. [Exeunt.]

ACT V

SCENE I

(Same as in Act IV. A Lieutenant, Jesper the Bailiff.)

LIEUTENANT. How can I manage to see the fellow, Mr. Bailiff? I should like to have a talk with him. Is he a likely looking fellow?

JESPER. Oh, he looks pretty well, and he has a mouth like a razor.

LIEUTENANT. That makes no difference, so long as he's strong and active.

JESPER. He can say anything he wants, and maintain it. He proved beyond a doubt that Peer the deacon was a cock.

LIEUTENANT. Is he good and broad across the shoulders?

JESPER. A big, strong lad. Every one in the house here is afraid of him, even his parents, for he can turn them into cows, oxen, and horses, then back again into people,--that is, he can prove that they are, from books.

LIEUTENANT. Does he look as if he could stand knocking about?

JESPER. And he proved that the earth was round, too.

LIEUTENANT. That doesn't matter to me. Does he look as if he were brave, and had a stout heart?

JESPER. He would stake his life for a letter of the alphabet, not to mention anything else. He has set every one here by the ears, but that makes no difference to him--he won't budge from his opinions and his learning.

LIEUTENANT. Mr. Bailiff, from all I hear, he will make a perfect soldier.

JESPER. How can you make a soldier of him, Lieutenant? He is a student.

LIEUTENANT. That has nothing to do with it. If he can turn people into sheep, oxen, and cocks, I'll have a try at turning a student into a soldier, for once.

JESPER. I should be happy if you could. I should laugh my belly in two.

LIEUTENANT. Just keep quiet about it, Jesper! When a bailiff and a lieutenant put their heads together, such things are not impossible. But I see some one coming this war. Is that he, by any chance?

JESPER. Yes, it is. I shall run off, so that he won't suspect me. [Exit.]

SCENE 2

(Enter Montanus.)

LIEUTENANT. Welcome to the village.

MONTANUS. I humbly thank you.

LIEUTENANT. I have taken the liberty of addressing you, because there aren't many educated people hereabouts for a man to talk to.

MONTANUS. I am delighted that you have been a scholar. When did you graduate, if I may inquire?

LIEUTENANT. Oh, ten years ago.

MONTANUS. Then you are an old academicus. What was your specialty when you were a student?

LIEUTENANT. I read mostly the old Latin authors, and studied natural law and moral problems, as in fact I do still.

MONTANUS. That is mere trumpery, not academicum. Did you lay no stress on Philosophiam instrumentalem?

LIEUTENANT. Not especially.

MONTANUS. Then you have never done any disputation?

LIEUTENANT. No.

MONTANUS. Well, is that studying? Philosophia instrumentalis is the only solid studium; the rest are all very fine, but they are not learned. One who is well drilled in Logica and Metaphysica can get himself out of any difficulty and dispute on all subjects, even if he is unfamiliar with them. I know of nothing which I should take upon myself to defend and not get out of it very well. There was never any disputation at the university in which I did not take part. A philosophus instrumentalis can pass for a polyhistor.

LIEUTENANT. Who is the best disputer nowadays?

MONTANUS. A student called Peer Iverson. When he has refuted his opponent so that he hasn't a word to say for himself, he says, "Now, if you will take my proposition, I will defend yours." In all that sort of thing his Philosophia instrumentalis is the greatest help. It is a shame that the lad did not become a lawyer; he could have made a mighty good living. Next to him, I am the strongest, for the last time I disputed, he whispered in my ear, "Jam sumus ergo pares." Yet I will always yield him the palm.

LIEUTENANT. But I have heard it said that Monsieur can prove that it is the duty of a child to beat his parents. That seems to be absurd.

MONTANUS. If I said it, I am the man to defend it.

LIEUTENANT. I dare wager a ducat that you are not clever enough for that.

MONTANUS. I will risk a ducat on it.

LIEUTENANT. Good. It is agreed. Now, let's hear you.

MONTANUS. He whom one loves most, he beats most. One ought to love nobody more than his parents, ergo there is nobody whom one ought to beat more. Now, in another syllogism: what one has received he ought, according to his ability, to return. In my youth I received blows from my parents. Ergo I ought to give them blows in return.

LIEUTENANT. Enough, enough, I have lost. Faith, you shall have your ducat.

MONTANUS. Oh, you were not in earnest; I will profecto take no money.

LIEUTENANT. Upon my word, you shall take it. I swear you shall.

MONTANUS. Then I will take it to keep you from breaking an oath.

LIEUTENANT. But may I not also try to turn you into something? Par exemple, I will turn you into a soldier.

MONTANUS. Oh, that is very easy, for all students are soldiers of the intellect.

LIEUTENANT. No, I shall prove that you are a soldier in body. Whoever has taken press-money is an enlisted soldier. You have done so, ergo--

MONTANUS. Nego minorem.

LIEUTENANT. Et ego probo minorem by the two rix-dollars you took into your hand.

MONTANUS. Distinguendum est inter nummos.

LIEUTENANT. No distinction! You are a soldier.

MONTANUS. Distinguendum est inter the two: simpliciter and relative accipere.

LIEUTENANT. No nonsense! The contract is closed, and you have taken the money.

MONTANUS. Distinguendum est inter contractum verum et apparentem.

LIEUTENANT. Can you deny that you have received a ducat from me?

MONTANUS. Distinguendum est inter rem et modum rei.

LIEUTENANT. Come, follow me straight, comrade! You must get your uniform.

MONTANUS. There are your two rix-dollars back. You have no witnesses to my taking the money.

SCENE 3

(Enter Jesper and Niels the Corporal.)

JESPER. I can bear witness that I saw the lieutenant put money into his hand.

NIELS. I too.

MONTANUS. But why did I take the money? Distinguendum est inter--

LIEUTENANT. Oh, we won't listen to any talk. Niels, you stay here, while I fetch the uniform. [Exit the Lieutenant.]

MONTANUS. Oh, help!

NIELS. If you don't shut up, you dog, I'll stick a bayonet through your body. Hasn't he enlisted, Mr. Bailiff?

JESPER. Yes, of course he has.

(Enter the Lieutenant.)

LIEUTENANT. Come, now, pull off that black coat and put on this red one. (Montanus cries while they put on his uniform.) Oh, come, it looks bad for a soldier to cry. You are far better off than you were before.--Drill him well, now, Niels. He is a learned fellow, but he is raw yet in his exercises. (Niels the Corporal leads Montanus about, drilling him and beating him.) [Exeunt the Lieutenant and Jesper.]

SCENE 4

(Enter the Lieutenant.)

LIEUTENANT. Well, Niels, can he go through the drill?

NIELS. He'll learn in time, but he is a lazy dog. He has to be beaten every minute.

MONTANUS (crying). Oh, gracious sir, have mercy on me. My health is weak and I cannot endure such treatment.

LIEUTENANT. It seems a little hard at first, but when your back has once been well beaten and toughened, it won't hurt so much.

MONTANUS (crying). Oh, would that I had never studied! Then I never should have got into this trouble.

LIEUTENANT. Oh, this is only a beginning. When you have sat a half score of times on the wooden horse, or stood on the stake, then you will think this sort of thing is a mere bagatelle. (Montanus weeps again.)

SCENE 5

(Enter Jeronimus, Magdelone, Jeppe, and Nille.)

JERONIMUS. Are you sure of it?

JEPPE. Indeed I am; the bailiff told me a moment ago. Ah, now my anger is turned to pity.

JERONIMUS. If we could only get him back to the true faith, I should be glad to buy him off.

LISBED (rushing in). Oh, poor wretch that I am!

JERONIMUS. Don't raise a hubbub, daughter, you won't gain anything by that.

LISBED. Oh, father dear, if you were as much in love as I am, you wouldn't ask me to keep quiet.

JERONIMUS. Fie, fie, it is not proper for a girl to show her feelings like that. But there he is, I do believe. Look here, Rasmus Berg! What is going on?

MONTANUS. Oh, my dear Monsieur Jeronimus, I've become a soldier.

JERONIMUS. Yes, now you have something else to do, besides turning men into beasts and deacons into cocks.

MONTANUS. Oh, alas! I lament my former folly, but all too late.

JERONIMUS. Listen, my friend. If you will give up your former foolishness, and not fill the land with disagreements and disputations, I shall not fail to do everything in my power to get you off.

MONTANUS. Oh, I don't deserve anything better, after threatening my old parents with blows. But if you will have pity on me and work for my release, I swear to you, that hereafter I shall live a different life, devote myself to some business, and never bother any one with disputations any more.

JERONIMUS. Stay here for a moment; I will go and talk to the Lieutenant. (Enter the Lieutenant.) Oh, my dear Lieutenant, you have always been a friend of our house. The person who has enlisted as a soldier is engaged to my only daughter, who is much in love with him. Set him free again. I shall be glad to present you with a hundred rix-dollars, if you do. I admit that at first I was delighted myself that he had been punished in such a way, for his singular behavior had exasperated me, and all the good folk here in the village, against him. But when I saw him in this plight, and at the same time heard him lament his former folly and promise amendment, my heart was ready to burst with sympathy.

LIEUTENANT. Listen, my dear Monsieur Jeronimus. What I have done has been only for his own good. I know that he is engaged to your daughter, and therefore merely for the good of your house I have reduced him to this condition and treated him with such great harshness, so that he might he brought to confess his sins. But for your sake I will give the money to the poor, inasmuch as I hear that he has experienced a change of heart. Let him come here.--Listen, my friend, your parents have spent much on you in the hope that you would become an honor and a comfort to them in their old age. But you go off a sensible fellow and come back entirely deranged, arouse the whole village, advance strange opinions, and defend them with stubbornness. If that is to be the fruit of studies, then one ought to wish that there never had been any books. It seems to me that the principal thing a man ought to learn in school is just the opposite of what you are infected with, and that a learned man ought particularly to be distinguished from others in that he is more temperate, modest, and considerate in his speech than the uneducated. For true philosophy teaches us that we ought to restrain and quiet disagreements, and to give up our opinions as soon as we are persuaded, even by the humblest person, that they are mistaken. The first rule of philosophy is, Know thyself; and the further one advances, the lower opinion one should have of himself, the more one should realize what there remains to be learned. But you make philosophy into a kind of fencing, and consider a man a philosopher if he can warp the truth by subtle distinctions and talk himself out of any opinion; in so doing you incur hatred and bring contempt upon learning, for people imagine that your extraordinary manners are the natural fruits of education. The best advice I can give you is to strive to forget, and to rid your head of what you have burned so much midnight oil in learning; and that you take up some calling in which you can make your way to success; or, if you are bound to pursue your studies, that you go about them in some other fashion.

MONTANUS. Oh, my good sir, I will follow your advice, and do my best to be a different man from now on.

LIEUTENANT. Good; then I will let you go as soon as you have given your word both to your own parents and to your future parents-in-law, and have begged their pardon.

MONTANUS. I humbly beg all of you, as I weep salt tears, to forgive me; and I promise to lead an entirely different life henceforward. I condemn my former ways, and I have been cured of them not so much by the fix I had got into as by this good man's wise and profound words. Next to my parents I shall always hold him in the highest esteem.

JERONIMUS. Then you don't believe any longer, my dear son-in-law, that the world is round? For that is the point that I take most to heart.

MONTANUS. My dear father-in-law, I won't argue about it any further. But I will only say this, that nowadays all learned folk are of the opinion that the earth is round.

JERONIMUS. Oh, Mr. Lieutenant, let him be made a soldier again until the earth becomes flat.

MONTANUS. My dear father-in-law, the earth is as flat as a pancake. Now are you satisfied?

JERONIMUS. Yes, now we are good friends again,--now you shall have my daughter. Come to my house, now, all together, and drink to the reconciliation. Mr. Lieutenant, won't you do us the honor of joining us?

www.bookjungle.com *email: sales@bookjungle.com fax: 630-214-0564 mail: Book Jungle PO Box 2226 Champaign, IL 61825*

The Codes Of Hammurabi And Moses
W. W. Davies

QTY

The discovery of the Hammurabi Code is one of the greatest achievements of archaeology, and is of paramount interest, not only to the student of the Bible, but also to all those interested in ancient history...

Religion   ISBN: *1-59462-338-4*   Pages:132
MSRP $12.95

The Theory of Moral Sentiments
Adam Smith

QTY

This work from 1749. contains original theories of conscience amd moral judgment and it is the foundation for systemof morals.

Philosophy   ISBN: *1-59462-777-0*   Pages:536
MSRP $19.95

Jessica's First Prayer
Hesba Stretton

QTY

In a screened and secluded corner of one of the many railway-bridges which span the streets of London there could be seen a few years ago, from five o'clock every morning until half past eight, a tidily set-out coffee-stall, consisting of a trestle and board, upon which stood two large tin cans, with a small fire of charcoal burning under each so as to keep the coffee boiling during the early hours of the morning when the work-people were thronging into the city on their way to their daily toil...

Childrens   ISBN: *1-59462-373-2*   Pages:84
MSRP $9.95

My Life and Work
Henry Ford

QTY

Henry Ford revolutionized the world with his implementation of mass production for the Model T automobile. Gain valuable business insight into his life and work with his own auto-biography... "We have only started on our development of our country we have not as yet, with all our talk of wonderful progress, done more than scratch the surface. The progress has been wonderful enough but..."

Biographies/   ISBN: *1-59462-198-5*   Pages:300
MSRP $21.95

www.bookjungle.com email: sales@bookjungle.com fax: 630-214-0564 mail: Book Jungle PO Box 2226 Champaign, IL 61825

The Art of Cross-Examination
Francis Wellman

QTY

I presume it is the experience of every author, after his first book is published upon an important subject, to be almost overwhelmed with a wealth of ideas and illustrations which could readily have been included in his book, and which to his own mind, at least, seem to make a second edition inevitable. Such certainly was the case with me; and when the first edition had reached its sixth impression in five months, I rejoiced to learn that it seemed to my publishers that the book had met with a sufficiently favorable reception to justify a second and considerably enlarged edition. ..

Reference   ISBN: *1-59462-647-2*   Pages:412 MSRP *$19.95*

On the Duty of Civil Disobedience
Henry David Thoreau

QTY

Thoreau wrote his famous essay, On the Duty of Civil Disobedience, as a protest against an unjust but popular war and the immoral but popular institution of slave-owning. He did more than write—he declined to pay his taxes, and was hauled off to gaol in consequence. Who can say how much this refusal of his hastened the end of the war and of slavery ?

Law   ISBN: *1-59462-747-9*   Pages:48 MSRP *$7.45*

Dream Psychology Psychoanalysis for Beginners
Sigmund Freud

QTY

Sigmund Freud, born Sigismund Schlomo Freud (May 6, 1856 - September 23, 1939), was a Jewish-Austrian neurologist and psychiatrist who co-founded the psychoanalytic school of psychology. Freud is best known for his theories of the unconscious mind, especially involving the mechanism of repression; his redefinition of sexual desire as mobile and directed towards a wide variety of objects; and his therapeutic techniques, especially his understanding of transference in the therapeutic relationship and the presumed value of dreams as sources of insight into unconscious desires.

Psychology   ISBN: *1-59462-905-6*   Pages:196 MSRP *$15.45*

The Miracle of Right Thought
Orison Swett Marden

QTY

Believe with all of your heart that you will do what you were made to do. When the mind has once formed the habit of holding cheerful, happy, prosperous pictures, it will not be easy to form the opposite habit. It does not matter how improbable or how far away this realization may see, or how dark the prospects may be, if we visualize them as best we can, as vividly as possible, hold tenaciously to them and vigorously struggle to attain them, they will gradually become actualized, realized in the life. But a desire, a longing without endeavor, a yearning abandoned or held indifferently will vanish without realization.

Self Help   ISBN: *1-59462-644-8*   Pages:360 MSRP *$25.45* www.bookjungle.com *email: sales@bookjungle.com fax: 630-214-0564 mail: Book Jungle PO Box 2226 Champaign, IL 61825*

QTY

- [ ] **The Rosicrucian Cosmo-Conception Mystic Christianity** *by Max Heindel* — ISBN: 1-59462-188-8 **$38.95**
  The Rosicrucian Cosmo-conception is not dogmatic, neither does it appeal to any other authority than the reason of the student. It is: not controversial, but is: sent forth in the, hope that it may help to clear..
  New Age/Religion Pages 646

- [ ] **Abandonment To Divine Providence** *by Jean-Pierre de Caussade* — ISBN: 1-59462-228-0 **$25.95**
  "The Rev. Jean Pierre de Caussade was one of the most remarkable spiritual writers of the Society of Jesus in France in the 18th Century. His death took place at Toulouse in 1751. His works have gone through many editions and have been republished...
  Inspirational/Religion Pages 400

- [ ] **Mental Chemistry** *by Charles Haanel* — ISBN: 1-59462-192-6 **$23.95**
  Mental Chemistry allows the change of material conditions by combining and appropriately utilizing the power of the mind. Much like applied chemistry creates something new and unique out of careful combinations of chemicals the mastery of mental chemistry...
  New Age Pages 354

- [ ] **The Letters of Robert Browning and Elizabeth Barret Barrett 1845-1846 vol II** — ISBN: 1-59462-193-4 **$35.95**
  by Robert Browning and Elizabeth Barrett
  Biographies Pages 596

- [ ] **Gleanings In Genesis (volume I)** *by Arthur W. Pink* — ISBN: 1-59462-130-6 **$27.45**
  Appropriately has Genesis been termed "the seed plot of the Bible" for in it we have, in germ form, almost all of the great doctrines which are afterwards fully developed in the books of Scripture which follow...
  Religion/Inspirational Pages 420

- [ ] **The Master Key** *by L. W. de Laurence* — ISBN: 1-59462-001-6 **$30.95**
  In no branch of human knowledge has there been a more lively increase of the spirit of research during the past few years than in the study of Psychology, Concentration and Mental Discipline. The requests for authentic lessons in Thought Control, Mental Discipline and...
  New Age/Business Pages 422

- [ ] **The Lesser Key Of Solomon Goetia** *by L. W. de Laurence* — ISBN: 1-59462-092-X **$9.95**
  This translation of the first book of the "Lernegton" which is now for the first time made accessible to students of Talismanic Magic was done, after careful collation and edition, from numerous Ancient Manuscripts in Hebrew, Latin, and French...
  New Age/Occult Pages 92

- [ ] **Rubaiyat Of Omar Khayyam** *by Edward Fitzgerald* — ISBN:1-59462-332-5 **$13.95**
  Edward Fitzgerald, whom the world has already learned, in spite of his own efforts to remain within the shadow of anonymity, to look upon as one of the rarest poets of the century, was born at Bredfield, in Suffolk, on the 31st of March, 1809. He was the third son of John Purcell...
  Music Pages 172

- [ ] **Ancient Law** *by Henry Maine* — ISBN: 1-59462-128-4 **$29.95**
  The chief object of the following pages is to indicate some of the earliest ideas of mankind, as they are reflected in Ancient Law, and to point out the relation of those ideas to modern thought.
  Religiom/History Pages 452

- [ ] **Far-Away Stories** *by William J. Locke* — ISBN: 1-59462-129-2 **$19.45**
  "Good wine needs no bush, but a collection of mixed vintages does. And this book is just such a collection. Some of the stories I do not want to remain buried for ever in the museum files of dead magazine-numbers an author's not unpardonable vanity..."
  Fiction Pages 272

- [ ] **Life of David Crockett** *by David Crockett* — ISBN: 1-59462-250-7 **$27.45**
  "Colonel David Crockett was one of the most remarkable men of the times in which he lived. Born in humble life, but gifted with a strong will, an indomitable courage, and unremitting perseverance...
  Biographies/New Age Pages 424

- [ ] **Lip-Reading** *by Edward Nitchie* — ISBN: 1-59462-206-X **$25.95**
  Edward B. Nitchie, founder of the New York School for the Hard of Hearing, now the Nitchie School of Lip-Reading, Inc, wrote "LIP-READING Principles and Practice". The development and perfecting of his meritorious work on lip-reading was an undertaking...
  How-to Pages 400

- [ ] **A Handbook of Suggestive Therapeutics, Applied Hypnotism, Psychic Science** — ISBN: 1-59462-214-0 **$24.95**
  by Henry Munro
  Health/New Age/Health/Self-help Pages 376

- [ ] **A Doll's House: and Two Other Plays** *by Henrik Ibsen* — ISBN: 1-59462-112-8 **$19.95**
  Henrik Ibsen created this classic when in revolutionary 1848 Rome. Introducing some striking concepts in playwriting for the realist genre, this play has been studied the world over.
  Fiction/Classics/Plays 308

- [ ] **The Light of Asia** *by sir Edwin Arnold* — ISBN: 1-59462-204-3 **$13.95**
  In this poetic masterpiece, Edwin Arnold describes the life and teachings of Buddha. The man who was to become known as Buddha to the world was born as Prince Gautama of India but he rejected the worldly riches and abandoned the reigns of power when...
  Religion/History/Biographies Pages 170

- [ ] **The Complete Works of Guy de Maupassant** *by Guy de Maupassant* — ISBN: 1-59462-157-8 **$16.95**
  "For days and days, nights and nights, I had dreamed of that first kiss which was to consecrate our engagement, and I knew not on what spot I should put my lips..."
  Fiction/Classics Pages 240

- [ ] **The Art of Cross-Examination** *by Francis L. Wellman* — ISBN: 1-59462-309-0 **$26.95**
  Written by a renowned trial lawyer, Wellman imparts his experience and uses case studies to explain how to use psychology to extract desired information through questioning.
  How-to/Science/Reference Pages 408

- [ ] **Answered or Unanswered?** *by Louisa Vaughan* — ISBN: 1-59462-248-5 **$10.95**
  Miracles of Faith in China
  Religion Pages 112

- [ ] **The Edinburgh Lectures on Mental Science (1909)** *by Thomas* — ISBN: 1-59462-008-3 **$11.95**
  This book contains the substance of a course of lectures recently given by the writer in the Queen Street Hail, Edinburgh. Its purpose is to indicate the Natural Principles governing the relation between Mental Action and Material Conditions...
  New Age/Psychology Pages 148

- [ ] **Ayesha** *by H. Rider Haggard* — ISBN: 1-59462-301-5 **$24.95**
  Verily and indeed it is the unexpected that happens! Probably if there was one person upon the earth from whom the Editor of this, and of a certain previous history, did not expect to hear again...
  Classics Pages 380

- [ ] **Ayala's Angel** *by Anthony Trollope* — ISBN: 1-59462-352-X **$29.95**
  The two girls were both pretty, but Lucy who was twenty-one who supposed to be simple and comparatively unattractive, whereas Ayala was credited, as her Bombwhat romantic name might show, with poetic charm and a taste for romance. Ayala when her father died was nineteen...
  Fiction Pages 484

- [ ] **The American Commonwealth** *by James Bryce* — ISBN: 1-59462-286-8 **$34.45**
  An interpretation of American democratic political theory. It examines political mechanics and society from the perspective of Scotsman James Bryce
  Politics Pages 572

- [ ] **Stories of the Pilgrims** *by Margaret P. Pumphrey* — ISBN: 1-59462-116-0 **$17.95**
  This book explores pilgrims religious oppression in England as well as their escape to Holland and eventual crossing to America on the Mayflower, and their early days in New England...
  History Pages 268

www.bookjungle.com email: sales@bookjungle.com fax: 630-214-0564 mail: Book Jungle PO Box 2226 Champaign, IL 61825

QTY

The Fasting Cure *by Sinclair Upton* ISBN: *1-59462-222-1* **$13.95**
In the Cosmopolitan Magazine for May, 1910, and in the Contemporary Review (London) for April, 1910, I published an article dealing with my experiences in fasting. I have written a great many magazine articles, but never one which attracted so much attention... New Age/Self Help/Health Pages 164

Hebrew Astrology *by Sepharial* ISBN: *1-59462-308-2* **$13.45**
In these days of advanced thinking it is a matter of common observation that we have left many of the old landmarks behind and that we are now pressing forward to greater heights and to a wider horizon than that which represented the mind-content of our progenitors... Astrology Pages 144

Thought Vibration or The Law of Attraction in the Thought World ISBN: *1-59462-127-6* **$12.95**
by William Walker Atkinson Psychology/Religion Pages 144

Optimism *by Helen Keller* ISBN: *1-59462-108-X* **$15.95**
Helen Keller was blind, deaf, and mute since 19 months old, yet famously learned how to overcome these handicaps, communicate with the world, and spread her lectures promoting optimism. An inspiring read for everyone... Biographies/Inspirational Pages 84

Sara Crewe *by Frances Burnett* ISBN: *1-59462-360-0* **$9.45**
In the first place, Miss Minchin lived in London. Her home was a large, dull, tall one, in a large, dull square, where all the houses were alike, and all the sparrows were alike, and where all the door-knockers made the same heavy sound... Childrens/Classic Pages 88

The Autobiography of Benjamin Franklin *by Benjamin Franklin* ISBN: *1-59462-135-7* **$24.95**
The Autobiography of Benjamin Franklin has probably been more extensively read than any other American historical work, and no other book of its kind has had such ups and downs of fortune. Franklin lived for many years in England, where he was agent... Biographies/History Pages 332

Name	
Email	
Telephone	
Address	
City, State ZIP	

☐ Credit Card   ☐ Check / Money Order

Credit Card Number	
Expiration Date	
Signature	

Please Mail to: Book Jungle
PO Box 2226
Champaign, IL 61825
or Fax to: 630-214-0564

ORDERING INFORMATION
web: *www.bookjungle.com*
email: *sales@bookjungle.com*
fax: *630-214-0564*
mail: *Book Jungle PO Box 2226 Champaign, IL 61825*
or PayPal *to sales@bookjungle.com*

Please contact us for bulk discounts

DIRECT-ORDER TERMS

20% Discount if You Order Two or More Books
Free Domestic Shipping!
Accepted: Master Card, Visa, Discover, American Express

www.ingramcontent.com/pod-product-compliance
Lightning Source LLC
Chambersburg PA
CBHW081833170426
43199CB00017B/2721